"When it comes to understanding prayer - the kind t[...] ...place that's deep and full of passion - I don't know that there s anyone with more to give than Dave Patterson. His life inspires me because it is a pursuit to know God and to live close to Him through prayer. I'm excited to see what God will do through this simple, straightforward and significant book."

DINO RIZZO, Co-founder and Executive Director of *ARC (Association of Related Churches)* and Associate Pastor, *Church of the Highlands*

"In over 15 years of ministry and serving the Church, I've never seen anyone so committed to ushering in the presence of God like Pastor Dave. His wisdom, experience, and insight have not only transformed our church, but in my life personally. We are using PURSUIT as a guide to take our church through every year."

BIANCA JUAREZ OLTHOFF, best-selling author and Lead Pastor, *The Father's House Orange County*

"I have seen in 50 years of ministry that prayer and fasting is the cornerstone of it all. I'm not smart enough to do what I do...I need serious help! Dave Patterson has modeled leaning on the Lord and birthed a dynamic and exploding ministry in Northern California on the same bedrock: "prayer and fasting." Buckle in with us. Walk forward 21 paces. Every pace will become a mile. Your entire year will change. I've proven it, Pastor Dave has proven it, and now it is time for ....YOU to prove it!"

LARRY STOCKSTILL, Founding Pastor and leader of *SURGE*

"I have known Pastor Dave Patterson for over a decade. His ability to preach the gospel in such a unique way allows people of all walks to understand the power of God! This devotional is exactly that! No matter where you are at in your relationship with God this devotional will easily take you to a new level!"

MATTHEW BARNETT, New York Times Best-Selling Author, Co-Founder of *The Dream Center*

PURSUIT

21-DAY
PRAYER & FASTING
DEVOTIONAL

DAVE PATTERSON

TFH

CONTENTS

PROLOGUE

THE 21-DAY GAME PLAN

This devotional will serve you best if you make a "**Pursuit** plan" and set aside a significant time each day to read, pray, write, and wait on God. Each chapter can be read in just a few minutes but the goal is not to see how quickly we can get through the content. The "win" is to use each chapter as a launching point for life-giving quality time with Jesus. I recommend the following tools in order to maximize your pursuit time:

- **A quiet, private place** where you can shut the door and be alone with the Lord (Psalm 91). I would also encourage you to find a place where you can lift your voice and cry out to God without worrying about who might hear you.

- **A Bible** you can highlight and write in.

- **A journal** to write out and process all that God will be saying.

- **Set aside time** in your day where you are mentally focused and undistracted. *(For many this time is in the morning before the business of the day takes over.)* The key is to "make an appointment with God" and don't miss it!

- **A great worship play-list.** This is the best way to ensure your pursuit time is "in the river" of God's presence.

Each chapter contains the following:

1. PLENTY OF SCRIPTURE

These are great passages for you to open up your bible and meditate on, read various translations, read the context, and highlight for future reference. The Word component is what releases the faith needed to continue our pursuit and to please God (Romans 10:17).

2. TAKE A MOMENT

In every chapter there will be a time where I ask you to take a moment to thank God, wait, listen, write down a thought, consider or call to memory a thought before moving on. Although it's just a moment, it will be important to take the recommended pauses as they are designed to be a Holy Spirit Selah' where a response is appropriate.

3. MEMORY VERSES

I encourage you to write down each day's verse so that you can take it with you to meditate on during the day. Build a reservoir of scriptures in your memory banks and The Holy Spirit will bring to your remembrance what you have invested into your mind. These verses will be arrows that you will draw out and use in future battles. Committing verses to memory takes time and focus. It is easy to neglect this precious discipline. If you have a hard time remembering the verses write them down on a sticky note or a flash card and place them around your house. But let me encourage you to take the time and put in the work to build your reservoir of verses in order to pray effectively and fight a good fight of faith! You'll never regret it.

4. PRAYER DIRECTIVE

This is different than taking a moment. This is where we shift gears from reading and journaling to spending some time lifting up our voices and passionately seeking God (James 5:16). The prayer directive is simply a runway to get your prayer motor started. I would encourage you to follow the Apostle Paul's admonition:

> *"I will pray in the spirit, and I will also pray in words I understand. I will sing in the spirit, and I will also sing in words I understand."*
>
> 1 CORINTHIANS 14:15

There are a variety of prayers listed and used in the Bible, from meditation to petition to intercession and many more. All of which are valuable at the right time and right application. I would encourage you to make your prayer time a place and space where you can mix it up and grow in all the different expressions of prayer.

5. THOUGHTS AND NOTES

This is the area to write down the things the Holy Spirit is bringing to light during your time with Him. My personal practice is to write it down as He is speaking, and then later on, I'll take some time to wait on God and will journal from those moments of revelation. The big idea is if you don't write it down, you'll lose it, just ask any songwriter. Let's be good stewards of the "rhema" (right now) words that are coming our way! After you've finished your ***Pursuit*** time you will be able to go back to your journal, to these moments of clarity and revelation, and will find new strength and prayer-fuel for the future!

PURSUIT

INTRODUCTION

For a couple decades now our church community, along with many churches around the nation, have been setting aside significant time in January, and other key seasons throughout the year, to pursue God through prayer and fasting. These are always significant times in our church and in the lives of individuals as we follow Jesus in this powerful, but often neglected, spiritual discipline. Jesus spoke of fasting as if it were a foregone conclusion that all of His disciples and future followers would make this a consistent practice in their lives. He said in Matthew chapter six:

*"...But when **you give**."*

*"...And when **you pray**."*

*"...and when **you fast**."*

These are the three non-negotiable components for a progressive life of power and abundance: Giving, praying and fasting. There is a long list of promises that are connected to a biblical fast and Isaiah 58 reveals that when we participate in the kind of fast that "God has chosen" we will not be able to outrun the inevitable returns. I want to invite you to set aside some days, or even weeks to pursue God in this time-tested way and then watch as these Isaiah 58 results start to come to pass in your life.

"....Then your light will break forth like the dawn, and your healing will quickly appear; then your righteousness will go before you, and the glory of the Lord will be your rear guard. Then you will call, and the Lord will answer; you will cry for help, and he will say: Here am I. "....then your light will rise in the darkness, and your night will become like the noonday. The Lord will guide you always; he will satisfy your needs in a sun-scorched land and will strengthen your frame. You will be like a well-watered garden, like a spring whose waters never fail."

ISAIAH 58:8-11

Pursuit, 21-Day devotional, is your invitation to pursue God through prayer and fasting in order to experience new levels of revelation, healing, power, intimacy with God. After 22 years of undertaking significant church-wide fasts, we've concluded that nothing takes the place of an all-out **Pursuit** of God. Pushing back the plate and running to your secret place of prayer is how you will see true breakthrough! I believe the following chapters will provide a daily dose of inspiration and motivation to help you dig deep. See what God will do as you pursue Him.

If you are new to the team and the spiritual discipline of fasting, I would encourage you to also check out "A Guide to Prayer and Fasting." Packed full of scripture, this short guide provides an explanation for the "why's" and "how's" of fasting.

Visit: *tfh.org/resources*

"Oh, that we might know the Lord!

Let us press on to know him.

He will respond to us as surely as the arrival of dawn

or the coming of rains in early spring."

HOSEA 6:3

Let's Go!

Dave Patterson

CHAPTER 1
THE PURSUIT

> " *For I know the plans I have for you,"*
> *declares the Lord, "plans to prosper you*
> *and not to harm you, plans to give you*
> *hope and a future. Then you will call on me*
> *and come and pray to me, and I will listen*
> *to you. **You will seek me and find me***
> ***when you seek me with all your heart.***
> *I will be found by you," declares the Lord."*
>
> JEREMIAH 29:11-13

WELCOME TO PURSUIT

Pursuit, a 21-day journey of pursuing Jesus through fasting and prayer. This devotional is centered on a promise that seems too good to be true, "You will seek me and find me when you seek me with all your heart" (Jeremiah 29:13). This is God's promise for those who set their hearts and lives in His direction, not looking back! When we seek God with all our hearts, we not only encounter Him but are changed by Him in the process. What a promise, especially considering that the Lord has never broken or failed to fulfill His Word!

Today we begin our days of prayer and fasting by standing on the firm foundation that we will never be disappointed in our **Pursuit** of God (Isaiah 49:23). During these valuable days of pursuing God, I believe you are going to discover things you've never known; you are going to receive new revelations, you will grow in your intimacy with Jesus, and you are going to encounter the power of God like never before!

GOD INITIATES DESIRE

I believe you have chosen to set aside this time of fasting and prayer because the Spirit has drawn you. Let me be clear that it is the Lord who initiates our **Pursuit** by drawing us first to Him and then giving us the desire to respond. Jesus said, "No one can come to me unless the Father who sent me draws them" (John 6:44). First, He draws, then He initiates desire, and by His grace, we respond.

TAKE A MOMENT

Thank God for drawing you to this place, this book, and this season of pursuing Him. Ask that He would increase the "draw" in you over these next 21-days; that there would be a deep longing to please and accomplish His will in your life. Just as Elisha asked for a double portion, be so bold as to ask for twice the hunger and thirst for His presence. According to Philippians 2:13, ask and believe that the Lord will create in you a deep and sustained longing to know and do His will.

"For it is not your strength, but it is God who is effectively at work in you, both to will and to work, that is, strengthening, energizing, and creating in you the longing and the ability to fulfill your purpose for His good pleasure."

PHILIPPIANS 2:13 (AMP)

OUR RESPONSE IS PURSUIT

Once we receive God's invitation and determine to run after Him, we set something in motion that can't be stopped. The enemy and your flesh would love to derail this time of intense **Pursuit** because it carries the promise and capacity to change your life and the lives of those around you. When you set your heart and passion to pursue God, the enemy is powerless to keep you from your destiny of breakthrough. Be aware that in the days ahead, you will need resilience, perseverance, and resolve. **The greater things of God are not for the casual observer** or those who audit church occasionally. The greater things of God are for those who have identified and ignited a holy resolve to seek God until!

DON'T STOP

This command needs to be so deeply ingrained in your Spirit that your default response to delays, trials, unanswered prayer, times of testing, or straight up spiritual attack is to stay in **Pursuit** mode! Don't stop asking, seeking, and knocking. This mindset and lifestyle are what will lead you to certain breakthrough and lasting change.

SEEK & FIND

*"For I know the plans I have for you," declares the Lord, "plans to prosper you and not to harm you, plans to give you hope and a future. Then you will call on me and come and pray to me, and I will listen to you. **You will seek me and find me** when you seek me with all your heart. I will be found by you," declares the Lord."*

JEREMIAH 29:11-13

"One day Jesus taught the apostles to keep praying and **never stop or lose hope."**

LUKE 18:1 (TPT)

"**Ask and keep on asking,** and it will be given to you; **seek and keep on seeking,** and you will find; **knock and keep on knocking,** and the door will be opened to you."

MATTHEW 7:7 (AMP)

Two key words stand out in this passage, **"seek"** and **"find."** Let's delve a little deeper.

1. To **seek** is, "to search for and not stop, to continue a quest until the object of our seeking has been obtained, and to create a well-worn path to the person or object we are in search of." We are embarking on a "with all your heart" journey of *Pursuit*. My prayer during these 21-days is that you would develop a spirit of seeking. That it would become such a part of who you are, that you will never again be satisfied with a lackluster approach to God or casual prayer life!

2. To **find** is "To be encountered, lighted upon, discovered. To run right into, gain possession of, and find sufficient." God promises that when we create a well-worn path to His presence, asking and seeking, we will, inevitably and most certainly find Him.

Is there anything greater than finding God? When we encounter Him, we discover new insights;

receive answers, healing, and direction; are filled with fresh passion and joy. THIS is the very essence and fullness of who God is! **There is nothing we need more in this life than to find and know God.** This is the quest you have embarked upon and the *Pursuit* you have started today.

The nature of faith is persistence and the language of faith is asking and continuing to ask "until."

> *"Then, teaching them more about prayer, he used this story: Suppose you went to a friend's house at midnight, wanting to borrow three loaves of bread. You say to him, 'A friend of mine has just arrived for a visit, and I have nothing for him to eat.' And suppose he calls out from his bedroom, 'Don't bother me. The door is locked for the night, and my family and I are all in bed. I can't help you.' But I tell you this—though he won't do it for friendship's sake, if you keep knocking long enough, he will get up and give you whatever you need **because of your shameless persistence.**"*

LUKE 11: 5-8

Jesus gave this illustration right after the disciples came to Him asking Him to teach them how to pray. Jesus then gave them the master template for prayer, which we now know as The Lord's prayer or the "Our Father." The continuation of his teaching on prayer revealed this non-negotiable element of "shameless persistence" and that the door would be opened if we would simply keep knocking. This is not a picture of God's resistance to answer prayer or His reluctance to bless His children. He delights in giving us good gifts, moving us into the abundant life He has already paid the price for. The reality is that there are demonic forces, we live on a broken planet, and there are elements that resist the will of God that require a determined, focused, persistent faith to break through.

STAY THE COURSE

There are going to be days where you may not feel like you've made headway, you have not received that download from heaven you were hoping for, and frankly, you don't feel emotionally pumped about what you've committed yourself to. At times like this remember that you are a man or women of faith. You know well the promises of God and have set your heart to be aligned with those promises. We are not moved by what we feel or by what we see, but by what we believe (2 Corinthians 5:7)!

Prepare your mind and heart to ask and keep asking, seek, and keep seeking, knock, and keep knocking. The moment you position yourself with this kind of resolve, you qualify to be one who will receive answers, discovering the deeper things of God, and moving through open doors!

MEMORY VERSE
*"You will seek me and find me
when you seek me with all your heart.
I will be found by you."*
JEREMIAH 29:13

PRAYER DIRECTIVE

Start out your prayer time by asking God to give you a new resilience and determination to "seek him until." Pray Matthew 7:7 and Jeremiah 29:13 out loud. Declare that you are stepping into a new season of whole-hearted *Pursuit* and you don't plan to back up or back off! Pray for a fuller revelation of His amazing promises and that a greater faith for this time of *Pursuit* would fill your heart and mind like never before.

THOUGHTS & NOTES

CHAPTER 2
CHOOSE YOUR WEAPON

It's very clear in scripture that we are all involved in a spiritual battle that is not an elective. The nature of this broken planet is such that spiritual forces are at work to limit our effectiveness, taking us out if possible. This presents the ever-present options of victory or defeat, fight or flee, breakthrough or breakdown. The difference between sustained victory or a defeated Christian life really comes down to our knowledge of and willingness to use the weapons of our warfare. New Testament writers frequently refer to our journey of faith as a battle or fight and they give us a right perspective of promised victory as we face these spiritual battles.

> *"For we are not fighting against flesh-and-blood enemies, but against evil rulers and authorities of the unseen world, against mighty powers in this dark world, and against evil spirits in the heavenly places."*
> EPHESIANS 6:12

> *"So, fight with faith for the winner's prize! Lay your hands upon eternal life, for this is your calling."*
> 1 TIMOTHY 6:12 (TPT)

> *"Be well balanced and always alert, because your enemy, the devil, roams around incessantly, like a roaring lion looking for its prey to devour. Take a decisive stand against him and resist his every attack with strong, vigorous faith."*
> 1 PETER 5:8-9 (TPT)

"For though we live in the world, we do not wage war as the world does. The weapons we fight with are not the weapons of the world. On the contrary, they have divine power to demolish strongholds."
2 CORINTHIANS 10:3-4

The problem, for many believers, is that they do not access or pick up the weapons that God has furnished for the battle! They've heard about the weapons, read books about the weapons, and could probably even tell you quite a bit about the arsenal, yet those very weapons lay in the dirt or neatly packed in the closet of their spiritual life.

I believe fasting is one of the most unused weapons in the arsenal of the believer. Many Christians know about fasting but somehow relegate it to first century Christians or some form of ancient asceticism (self-imposed suffering to gain God's approval).

RIDICULOUS WEAPONS

If you were to examine many of the battle plans in scripture, you would find that the strategies used, and weapons employed, seemed a bit ridiculous. For example, when King Jehoshaphat and the people of Israel were about to be attacked by a vast army, they picked up a few weapons that seemed a bit "ridiculous" yet yielded a miraculous victory. Their weapons of choice were to fast and sing (2 Chronicles 20). Now, what kind of army would weaken their soldiers with fasting, and then send in an unarmed choir to the frontlines of the battle? Yet, that's what King Jehoshaphat did.

Fasting is a powerful weapon for your use and advantage today!

Sure, it doesn't make sense to the carnal mind, yet Jesus told us that some forms of breakthrough and freedom **only** *come by prayer and fasting.*

(SEE MATHEW 17:21)

Singing, "Give thanks to the Lord, for his love endures forever" the choir and army marched into battle. This God-given lyric, a simple yet powerful weapon, led the way to Israel's triumph. Scripture tells us that because of King Jehoshaphat's simple and even ridiculous strategy the location of the battle was permanently changed to "The Valley of Blessing." **God turned a valley of imminent destruction into a valley of blessing through the simplicity of praise!** "God brought about a great victory that day." And so, it is with you and your journey of faith. During these 21-days of *Pursuit* I encourage you to pick up the unused weapons of your arsenal, and then watch as the Lord fights for you.

WEAPONS OF WARFARE

We could define a spiritual weapon as "anything found in scripture that drives back the powers of darkness, defeats our spiritual enemies, and establishes the Kingdom of Heaven here on earth." Based on that description, here are several weapons found in the word (not an all-inclusive list):

- PRAYER
- INTERCESSION *(focused prayer for others)*
- THANKSGIVING
- SINGING
- GIVING
- TITHING
- TIME IN THE SECRET PLACE
- UNITY
- PRAISE
- COMMUNION
  (OBSERVING THE TABLE OF THE LORD)
- MEMORIZING SCRIPTURE
  (BATTLE GROUND OF THE MIND)
- FORGIVING OTHERS
- RESOLVING OFFENSE
- DECLARING THE WORD
- BINDING AND LOOSING
- FASTING

Whether it's giving, fasting, singing or simply telling someone you are sorry, when we intentionally use these simple weapons it activates things in the spirit realm that cannot be accessed any other way. God uses the simple to confound the wise!

(SEE 1 CORINTHIANS 1:27)

TAKE A MOMENT

Go over the list of spiritual weapons we have provided and do a quick inventory of which weapons you are consistently using, and which ones are laying on the ground, gathering dust or perhaps have never even found their way into your arsenal. Then consider how you can take up some new weapons during this **Pursuit**. For those of you who are new to fasting, let me encourage you to go after God with a biblical fast and see what He will do.

BIG PROMISES

Let's return to our key passage for a moment. In 2 Corinthians 10:4 it says that "these weapons have divine power to demolish strongholds." This is a huge promise and reality. When we fight God's way and with His weapons, demonic forces, strongholds, and barriers are not just pushed back, delayed or discouraged, they are destroyed! If you've ever seen video of an old building being demolished, that's what the Hebrew word means. This is the power available when we utilize the weapons we've been given. Those fortresses of despair or barricades of unworthiness that have limited your future in God are on the brink of being blown to bits as you step into this season of fasting and prayer!

STRATEGY IS IMPORTANT

When it comes to construction, or any trade, working plans and the right tools at the right time make all the difference and so it is with the weapons or "tools" of our warfare. Once King David was inquiring of the Lord as to how and when to attack the Philistines who were coming to capture him (2 Samuel 5:17-25). The Lord instructed him to go straight at them and guaranteed that David and the armies of Israel would see victory. Sure enough! God broke through the enemy's forces like a flood of water, so David named the place Baal-perazim (which means "the Lord who bursts through"). But after a while the Philistine armies recovered and returned to attack once again (a very real picture of our spiritual enemies). David did not presume victory based on past successes but sought God again for the right strategy, to which God replied *"'Do not attack them straight on,' the Lord replied. 'Instead, circle around behind and attack.'"*

2 SAMUEL 5:23

*"...And **I will rebuke the devourer** for your sakes, so that he will not destroy the fruit of your ground."*

MALACHI 3:11

We can learn well from David's example. Some battles require fasting, others a shout of victory, sometimes a prayer of agreement, or practicing radical generosity. Other times the massive ground we are attempting to claim can be gained by simply humbling ourselves and saying "I'm sorry." The key to consistent forward movement and progress is to; always seek God first, be willing and ready to be obedient, be led by the Spirit and use the right weapon at the right time.

MEMORY VERSE
*"The weapons we fight are not
the weapons of the world.
On the contrary, they have divine power
to demolish strongholds."*
2 CORINTHIANS 10:4

PRAYER DIRECTIVE

As we spend time with the Lord, let's ask Him to reveal to us the weapons that we have neglected or perhaps have yet to discover. Ask Him to show you what the battle plan is for this time of *Pursuit*. Strategy is as important as our willingness to fight. God is the one who releases divine strategy as we wait on Him. Ask the Lord if there is a specific weapon that you need to use today. It might even look like a "ridiculous" weapon, but who knows, you could be a simple song away from breakthrough.

THOUGHTS & NOTES

CHAPTER 3
PREPARING FOR POWER

Jesus talked about giving, praying, and fasting as if they were non-negotiable practices in the life of a believer. Yet, wrong motivations for these spiritual disciplines can derail the results, turning them into meaningless religious routines.

*"So, **when you give** to the needy, do not announce it with trumpets, as the hypocrites do...And **when you pray**, do not be like the hypocrites...And **when you fast**, don't make it obvious, as the hypocrites do."*

MATTHEW 6:2,5 & 16

The religious leaders of Jesus' day, those he kept referring to as "hypocrites," prayed publicly, gave more money at the synagogue than the average person, and fasted two days a week! Sounds like a pretty serious commitment that you would think God would be impressed with and respond to. However, Jesus said the only reward they would receive was the admiration of people. I don't know about you, but I'm looking for quite a bit more than impressing people in my pursuit of God! The key to fasting effectively and praying prayers that move heaven are to:

- ## SPEND SIGNIFICANT TIME IN THE SECRET PLACE

  The secret place is simply that undistracted, designated place of prayer and worship that you intentionally reserve for just you and the Lord. This is where we go and "shut the door" to meet with God in secret. Jesus made us a promise when we do this: *"But whenever you pray, go into your innermost chamber and be alone with Father God, praying to him in secret. And **your Father, who sees all you do, will reward you** openly."*
  MATTHEW 6:6 (TPT)

  My prayer for you is that you would increase your life in the secret place and develop a stronger desire to be a "one thing" pursuer of God!

  *"**Here's the one thing** I crave from God, the one thing I seek above all else: I want the privilege of living with him every moment in his house, finding the sweet loveliness of his face, filled with awe, delighting in his glory and grace. I want to live my life so close to him that he takes pleasure in my every prayer."*
  PSALM 27:4 (TPT)

- ## BE LED BY THE SPIRIT

  We will talk about the secret place in an upcoming chapter, so let's consider your ***Pursuit*** in light of being led by the Spirit. If we're not careful, the term "Spirit-led" can get ethereal and spooky, leading many down a road of subjective behavior and charismania, yet the Word is clear that this is how we are to navigate our spiritual lives.

"The mature children of God are those who are moved (led) by the impulses of the Holy Spirit."

ROMANS 8:14 (TPT)

Let's consider Jesus' preparation for ministry as he fasted for forty days and forty nights in the wilderness.

*"Jesus, full of the Holy Spirit, left the Jordan and **was led by the Spirit into the wilderness**, where for forty days he was tempted by the devil. He ate nothing during those days, and at the end of them he was hungry."* LUKE 4:1-2

There are a couple of questions worth considering from this passage. First, does the Spirit actually lead you into times of testing and a wilderness experience in order to release you into a new season of power and realized potential? Second, what kind of fast is the Spirit leading you into? Third, what should you expect during these days of ***Pursuit***? There are no biblical mandates or verse by verse instructions detailing how long we should fast, how often or what type of fast we should undertake. So, we will need to seek God for clarity and direction as to what our days of ***Pursuit*** will look like. Then, we simply follow the Spirit's leading. I have had the Spirit lead me into three-day fasts, fourteen-day fasts and once, during a crucial time of ministry re-direction in my life, a 40-day fast. I would recommend getting some counsel and confirmation from trusted leaders and spiritual mentors for any extended time of fasting. If we get caught up trying to break a personal record or focus on doing what others are doing, fasting can turn into a religious routine that resembles the methods of the Pharisees. At the same time, we should not avoid the practice of fasting because we do not "feel led." Fasting is a discipline and an act of faith that we can initiate whenever we choose.

*So, **buckle up** and get your mind set in the right place so that you can see it through to the end.*

TAKE A MOMENT

Ask the Holy Spirit what your time of **Pursuit** should look like. How long should you fast, and what type of fast will you commit to undertaking? Do you sense the grace and passion to go for it? If you will wait on God and are willing to do whatever He leads you to do, it will become apparent. Once you have clarified what the Holy Spirit is leading you to do, **be sure not to let your flesh or appetite determine the *Pursuit*.** Be lead by the Holy Spirit within you as you set aside your agenda and succumb to God's direction. As you do this, you will find resolve and grace to go the distance while discovering a new level of faith for the days ahead.

- **THIS WAS NOT ON THE BROCHURE**

   The next step is to prepare your mind and Spirit for what might happen as the Spirit leads you in these days. Many have a romantic concept of fasting and anticipate dreams, visions, angelic visitations, and an immediate sense of being closer to God than they ever have before. In my experience, this is not always the case. Don't get me wrong, fasting does create a nearness to Jesus and a sensitivity to the Spirit that nothing else will produce, but oftentimes during a fast, we will deal with some heart issues that begin to surface. We will be confronted with our baggage and bondage that God is longing to free us from or will face some real external spiritual opposition as we pursue God.

Let's consider Jesus again:

"He was led by the Spirit in the wilderness, where he was tempted by the devil for forty days."
LUKE 4:1-2

This is the part that is not in the brochure! Who signs up for a wilderness trip to be tempted and have a one-on-one confrontation with the Prince of Darkness? This doesn't sound like my idea of a spiritual retreat! But, let's look at the end-game.

There were four distinct dynamics that happened to Jesus during his time of fasting that I believe we can use as template during any season of an extended fast. This will help us to have realistic expectations and to not be derailed as we encounter resistance and warfare in the process.

1. WE WILL DEVELOP A DEEP & COMPLETE DEPENDENCE ON THE SUSTAINING STRENGTH OF GOD.

    "Man shall not live on bread alone, but on every word that comes from the mouth of God."

    MATTHEW 4:4

2. WE WILL LEARN HOW TO FIGHT WITH THE SWORD OF THE SPIRIT.

    "It is written... it is written... it is written!"

    MATTHEW 4:1-11

3. WE WILL LEARN TO RESIST AND DEFEAT THE DEVIL.

    "Get out of here, Satan," Jesus told him. "For the Scriptures say, 'You must worship the Lord your God and serve only him.'" Then the devil went away."

    MATTHEW 4:10

4. WE WILL RETURN OR CONCLUDE OUR FAST IN THE POWER OF THE SPIRIT.

    There is something in this portion of scripture that I want you to see and never forget. **Jesus headed into the wilderness full of the Spirit, but he returned in the power of the Spirit!** There is a direct and obvious connection between fasting and the empowerment, the wilderness battle and the start of his miraculous, public ministry where demons cried out as he approached, and healings flowed freely to all who were near him.

*"Then Jesus, **being filled with the Holy Spirit**, returned from the Jordan and was led by the Spirit into the wilderness."*
LUKE 4:1

*"Then Jesus **returned in the power of the Spirit** to Galilee, and news of Him went out through all the surrounding region."*
LUKE 4:14

I believe these days of ***Pursuit*** are setting you up for a new release of power and authority in your life! If Jesus needed to fast to see a release of power, then so do we. We have the biblical example of the "non-fasting" disciples who lacked power as the negative illustration of this truth (see Matthew 21:19-21).

Before we pray, I want to remind you of the words of the Apostle Paul who lived a life of fasting, while being used consistently by the power of God. This verse will also serve as our memory verse for the day.

MEMORY VERSE

"My message and my preaching were not with wise and persuasive words, but with a demonstration of the Spirit's power, so that your faith might not rest on human wisdom, but on God's power."

1 CORINTHIANS 2:4

PRAYER DIRECTIVE

Today as you spend some time with the Lord, ask the Holy Spirit to lead you into and through every day of your *Pursuit.* That when you face the powers of hell you won't be discouraged or surprised but will be prepared to wield the sword of the Word!

Let the Word of God be your sword as you resist and defeat your personal enemies. Ask for a fresh baptism of fire and power so that you can be fully prepared for the ministry that awaits you as you "return in the power."

THOUGHTS & NOTES

CHAPTER 4
GOD IS LOOKING

One of the areas we will be focusing on during our time of **Pursuit** is our prayer and intercession for others. It is powerful, inspiring, overwhelming, and border-line unbelievable that our prayers can change the course of someone's life, the spiritual climate of a city, or the destiny of a nation! And yet, it's true! Your prayers have the capacity to release great power and can be a game changer for those who cannot or will not pray for themselves.

What is intercession exactly? Intercession means to "stand between" or "to go in behalf of." This is what Jesus has done and continues to do for us! "Therefore, he is able to save completely those who come to God through him, because he always lives to intercede for them" Hebrews 7:25. As Jesus intercedes for us, He is standing between the brokenness of humanity and the needed grace and mercy of the Father. He has released the church, you and I, to be involved in this same ministry. *"Most of all, I'm writing to encourage you to pray with gratitude to God. Pray for all men with all forms of prayers and requests as you intercede with intense passion."* 1 TIMOTHY 2:1(TPT)

The Greek word for intercession, 'pagha,' means "to make a petition or conversation on behalf of another," or "to go to God representing another." According to Ezekiel 22:30 this is called **standing in the gap.**

The "gap" is a place between the mess of humanity and the much-needed grace and intervention of God. God is looking for people to boldly approach the throne of God, making petitions on **behalf of others**. The purpose and need for intercessors are to justify divine intervention. Remember that God operates with perfect justice. He has set into motion the laws of sowing and reaping. It is a rare scriptural exception for God to override people's free-will or overturn the set law of reaping the appropriate harvest that has been determined by the seeds sown (see Galatians 6:7-8).

In order to release the best over those who deserve the worst, God has set into motion a spiritual law or principle that interrupts the set process of sowing and reaping. This is the law of intercession. We see this in 2 Chronicles 7:14, "If my people, who are called by my name will…" Let's stop right there; the operative words in this famous passage are *"if"* and *"will."* The promise God is making is contingent upon intercession for a nation that is deserving of judgment, yet God is saying, "I'm providing another way, a path of rescue and redemption."

Let's back up a verse and read the context of this famous passage, *"When I shut up the heavens so that there is no rain or command locusts to devour the land or send a plague among my people."*
2 CHRONICLES 7:13

The only reason God would send or allow those destructive things to happen to His people is that, in alignment with His perfect justice, the time of judgment has come.

God has set into motion a law that is higher than the law of sowing and reaping; the law of intercession!

"I looked for someone among them who would build up the wall and stand before me in the gap on behalf of the land so I would not have to destroy it, but I found no one."

EZEKIEL 22:30

What a powerful thought! God is telling us that our intercession can actually hold back the harvest of destruction and judgment and release grace instead. That when rebellion, sin and disobedience call for a harvest of pain and loss we can see that delayed and even overturned as we "stand in the gap" This should motivate us to pray and never quit.

GOD IS LOOKING FOR YOU

One powerful line that jumps out of the Ezekiel passage is, ".... and I searched for a man." God is looking for intercessors. He is searching for those who are willing to pray selflessly for others until breakthrough comes. Right before Jesus rescued my life I was bound in addiction, deception and headed down a dismal road that would have certainly ended in a premature death. But while I was unable and unwilling to pray for myself an amazing woman of God in our church went on a 14-day fast for my freedom and rescue. She called other intercessors and led a "rescue campaign" for my future. I truly believe that her sacrifice and willingness to **"stand in the gap"** for me was the turning point in my life!

If you have been searching for God, let me encourage you to position your life where you are sure to meet with him consistently. You do this by becoming the person, the prayer warrior, the intercessor that He is already searching for. Everyone can do this! Anyone can volunteer, step up, and take the role of the intercessor. Some people have referred to themselves or others as having "the gift of intercession" but **nowhere in the Bible is intercession seen as a spiritual gift, exclusive calling, or a special burden for a select few.** Yes, some indeed intercede with greater anointing and authority, which I believe develops through proximity, availability, and intimacy; yet we are all invited to stand in the gap praying powerful prayers for others!

Remember this powerful truth: **"Intercession justifies divine intervention."**

Stand in the gap!

TAKE A MOMENT

Who was praying for you when you could not or would not pray for yourself? I would bet that you could trace your road to salvation or freedom back to the prayers of someone who prayed selflessly for you during your darkest days. So, who are you standing for now? Who is on your heart and mind right now as you read these words? Do you feel the compassion of Jesus for them? Can you see their face and imagine them standing in the presence of God again, wholly changed by His grace? Consider this your official invitation to stand in the gap for them.

PRAY WITH PASSION

There is something that happens as we decide to pray for someone "until." When we pray with intensity and resolve, asking God to allow us to feel what he feels and to see them the way He does, our passion level will rise. We will start to carry a burden for those we are interceding for. A burden is not a negative thing but is a gift from God's heart that fills ours. This will take us to places in prayer where we pray with passion, emotion, and see the power of God released. As you pray for your family and close friends whose lives are being destroyed by a very real enemy, allow your heart to break the way our Heavenly Father's does. Spend the time required, asking God to let you feel what He feels for them and then let the love and purpose of God be released through your prayers. This kind of praying can become emotional and even intense in its expression, thus pray in the secret place where you can be free to do what it takes to pray these effective prayers of passion.

MEMORY VERSE
"Tremendous power is released through the passionate, heartfelt prayer of a godly believer."
JAMES 5:16 (TPT)

PRAYER DIRECTIVE

During your time of **Pursuit**, ask God to take you to a place of passionate, heartfelt prayer. Go beyond mere words and human understanding of the need. Go to where you are feeling His heart and release passion into the situation!

Take a few minutes to write down the names of the top 3-5 people in your world who cannot or will not pray for themselves. Make a determination to stand in the gap for them until they encounter the grace of God and the life-change they so desperately need. As you pray, ask the Lord to give you his heart and compassion for them, and ask the Holy Spirit to enable you to stay in this place of prayer until significant work has been done.

THOUGHTS & NOTES

CHAPTER 5
RESILIENCE REQUIRED

"
Most people quit too soon!"

I remember when Donna and I first went into ministry. We were traveling up and down the West Coast with a band of musicians, believing God for big things. After a couple of years without significant breakthrough or success in our "Contemporary Christian Music Career" I was discouraged, disillusioned and pretty much convinced I should lay down my guitar, pick up a hammer, and go back into construction. During this season of discouragement, we were speaking at a small church, and the pastor came to me after the meeting and said something that has stuck with me for over thirty years. After I shared some of my dismal outlook with him, he looked me in the eye and said, "Son, you'll be amazed at what God will do with your life if you'll determine to just keep showing up" and then he walked away. I've never forgotten that moment.

So, for the next three-plus decades of ministry and life, that's exactly what I've been doing, just showing up. I'm never the smartest guy in the room, definitely not the most gifted, educated or best looking, but here's one thing you should know about me: I'm going to show up! I keep showing up to the prayer meeting, showing up to prepare the Word, showing up when the worship service starts, showing up to serve where I'm needed, just showing up!

Come to find out; this is one of the most powerful principles you can embrace and live out. It will change the way you view prayer, ministry, and many aspects of your life! **Don't quit in the middle, don't lay down during the battle, and don't walk away from your field while the seed is still in the ground.** Ask God for a long-term perspective and a Holy resilience to stand and pray until.

One of the main reasons our church and many other churches all over the nation engage in 21 days of fasting and prayer is because of the example set by a young man named Daniel in Babylon around 600 BC. Daniel was determined to stay loyal to Jehovah, not defiling himself with all the perks of being hand-picked by King Nebuchadnezzar to serve in his royal service. This resolve to take a stand for God, and thus against the culture and king of a wicked nation, quickly put him into a test of his faith that he and three of his Hebrew buddies would have to walk out. His three friends were bound with ropes and thrown into a fire. Yet God was with them in the fire, and they came through and came out with more authority and confidence than when they started. This seems to be true of all fiery tests. Daniel was tossed into a pit of lions to be the appetizer for the night, but God had other plans. Fast forward, the years in captivity are clipping by and Daniel realizes that the seventy years of captivity of the Children of Israel are coming to a close. This meant that the prophecy of their deliverance was about to come to pass, thus releasing God's people, Daniel and his buddies from their current situation. But God's people had not kept their part of the covenant thus potentially forfeiting the promise of God for deliverance. They sinned, rebelled against God, scorned His commands and regulations, and refused to listen to His servants the prophets (see Daniel 9:5-6).

So, Daniel decided to seek God through prayer and fasting...

So, Daniel decided to seek God through prayer and fasting. He determined that he would undertake a customized fast for 21 days and pray three times a day for God's mercy on the nation and the deliverance of his people.

TAKE A MOMENT

Consider how our country has turned away from its heritage as a Christian nation and how many churches have embraced the broken values of a fallen culture. Use Daniel's prayer to pray for the Church and our nation. Pray for revival, fresh conviction, a new move of the Holy Spirit, for life-giving churches to rise up, and that God would lean down and smile again.

Following is Daniel's prayer over the nation that "bears God's name."

> *"O our God hear your servant's prayer! Listen as I plead. For your own sake, Lord, smile again on your desolate sanctuary. O my God, lean down and listen to me. Open your eyes and see our despair. See how your city—the city that bears your name—lies in ruins. We make this plea, not because we deserve help, but because of your mercy. O Lord, hear. O Lord, forgive. O Lord listen and act! For your own sake, do not delay, O my God, for your people and your city bears your name."*
>
> DANIEL 9:17-20

*Remember, praying with faith, when in alignment with the promises of God, **always produces results!***

Daniel set himself to seek God, to repent and "stand in the gap" for his nation. While he is praying, he has a visitation and a word from God that I want you to embrace as your own: **"The moment you began praying, a command was given"** (Daniel 9:23).

This message was given to Daniel before he started his fast. He was headed into a time of pursuit, and God was letting him know that as soon as he set his heart to seek the Lord that something was set in motion, and so it is with you! When we get serious about pursuing God for a spiritual breakthrough, renewal, revival, the restoration of our nation, and the salvation of others, something is set in motion!

Daniel fasted for 21 days and prayed three times a day during his fast. At the end of his fast he has another visitation from God. Whether this is an angel or a Christophany is a theological discussion we will leave for another day, but God meets with him and tells him something you and I need to hear:

> *"Then he said, "Don't be afraid, Daniel. **Since the first**
> **day you began to pray** for understanding and to humble
> yourself before your God, your request has been heard
> in heaven. I have come in answer to your prayer. **But**
> **for twenty-one days** the spirit prince of the kingdom of
> Persia **blocked my way.**"*
>
> DANIEL 10:12-13

Although Daniel's prayer was heard on day one, and a response was set in motion, there were 21 days of resistance. While Daniel fasted and prayed, there was warfare happening in the heavens that he could not see and knew nothing about. And so, it is with our times of intense pursuit. There is a very real and ever-present spiritual battle that is being waged that requires resilience and persistence on our part if we are going to see the breakthrough and the move of God that we are crying out for. Now, if you are praying for a better parking spot at the mall or to find your lost sock I doubt there will be any demonic resistance involved, but when we set our hearts to see a move of God in our city, to see the lost come home and the bound set free, be prepared for resistance. Yet we wait in faith, we fast in faith, and we understand that we **win if we don't quit!**

MEMORY VERSE
"Then Jesus told his disciples a
parable to show them that they
should always pray and not give up."

LUKE 18:1

PRAYER DIRECTIVE

Ask God to put a resilience in your spirit that will enable you to stand in faith like Daniel and believe like Abraham! Let's ask God for insight into the spiritual realms that we might understand the scope of what we are battling for and the need for faith and patience in the middle of the fight.

Ask God to give you a passion in prayer that will enable to you *"always pray and never give up."* You will be amazed at what God will do with your life if you'll determine to just keep showing up.

THOUGHTS & NOTES

CHAPTER 6
A HEARING EAR

"
So then faith comes by hearing,
and hearing by the word of God."

ROMANS 10:17 (NKJV)

This is review for most, so as a reminder, the word for hearing in this familiar verse is 'rhema' which means, "That which is uttered by the living voice." For our prayer application today, ***it's not merely what has been said or written, but what God is saying right now that produces faith***, resulting in powerful prayers. Jesus told us that his sheep would hear and recognize His voice (see John 10:27). We can come into His presence with confidence knowing that He desires to speak to our hearts, and when we hear His voice dynamic faith ignites!

If you've walked with God for any period of time you realize how priceless and unique it is when the Lord speaks with clarity and certainty. I can testify that the most significant decisions and adventures of faith in my life, including marrying my wife and starting a church, came about as the direct result of hearing from God. I am so glad I did both! When we genuinely know God's desire for our future, and His remedy for our particular problem or situation, we can then pray with faith and certainty.

God speaks to everyone in different ways, times and seasons but two common denominators can be found for those who are in consistent two-way communication:

- ## THEY HEAR FROM GOD IN THE CONTEXT OF HIS WORD.

  The impressions, whispers, God-thoughts, or inner voice conversations will always be in alignment with and flow from what God has already said. One sure way of having increased, consistent communication with the Holy Spirit is to stay in the Word! Study the Word, meditate on the Word, and treasure the Word. This is the Lord's primary mode of communication with us.

- ## THEY HAVE DEVELOPED A HEARING EAR.

  There is a promise in Isaiah that I want you to receive as your own today, *"Whether you turn to the right or to the left, your ears will hear a voice behind you, saying, 'This is the way; walk in it.'"*
  ISAIAH 30:21

  What a promise! No matter what we are facing, no matter how complicated the situation or high the risk, if we will hear the voice of God then we have the guarantee of clear direction. In light of this scriptural truth, it would make perfect sense that **the enemy's greatest and most effective weapons against us are distraction, confusion, a multiplicity of voices, and the inability to be still and listen.**

  Today, consider the value of being still before God in light of the promise of hearing His voice when you wait in His presence. If hearing from God clearly and unmistakably is

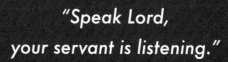

new territory for you, we are going to learn from a young man named Samuel who had his first conversation with God. You can read the full story in 1 Samuel Chapter 3.

> *"One night Eli, who was almost blind by now, had gone to bed. The lamp of God had not yet gone out, and Samuel was sleeping in the Tabernacle near the Ark of God. Suddenly the Lord called out, 'Samuel!' 'Yes?' Samuel replied. 'What is it?' He got up and ran to Eli. 'Here I am. Did you call me?'"*
> 1 SAMUEL 3:2-5

This was Samuels first encounter with hearing the voice of God and the starting point for two-way communication with God. Hearing the voice of God was so foreign to Samuel that he mistook God's voice as that of his mentor and boss, Eli, the priest. After a couple of failed attempts to connect with God, Eli instructed Samuel to go lay down and when he hears the voice a third time to respond by saying, "Speak Lord, your servant is listening."

TAKE A MOMENT

Like Samuel, pray this out loud, *"Speak Lord, your servant is listening."* Quiet your heart and focus on His goodness and His desire to reveal himself to you. Let God know that he has your full attention. I find it best to have a tablet of paper, journal, or recording device readily available when I do this.

Never underestimate the power of one clear sentence straight from the heart of God.

————

Remember, hearing clearly is a matter of proximity.

NOW, BACK TO SAMUEL

Once Samuel understood who was speaking to him, and how to respond, he received a message that would not only change his life but the life of his nation. I have had the direction of my life completely change with just a few clear words of guidance from the Lord.

There is a lot we can learn from Samuel's story, increasing our ability to hear the voice of God more clearly and consistently:

- **STAY NEAR THE PRESENCE**
  Verse 3 tells us that Samuel was sleeping in the Tabernacle near the Ark of God. What a beautiful picture, to be resting right there in the very presence of God. This speaks to us of the need to have a heart of worship, and to find a place of intimate, uninterrupted conversation.

  Once you experience the presence of God, don't be in a hurry to move on. Make sure your ***Pursuit*** time involves plenty of worship and adoration with no agenda other than to draw close (James 4:8).

This reality carries on beyond your secret place and personal devotion. Many times, you will hear from God while standing with hundreds or thousands of worshippers. The key is be where a true and powerful river of worship is flowing! Be willing to make the investment of time to go where the worshippers are gathered as well as create a place of private worship where you can be in the presence of God with consistency.

• LAY DOWN AND WAIT

It might not be crucial to get down in the prone position, but it never hurts. The idea is to find a place that is free of distraction so that you can quiet your mind and heart. Prayer is designed to be a dialogue, not a monologue. If we only present our praise, rattle off requests, and then head out the door we are missing the most important moment of our *Pursuit* time, hearing God's response. There is much to be said and great books have been written on hearing from God. For this devotional let's simply make this point: hearing from God requires that we silence other voices, quiet our souls, and cease from striving (i.e. emails, calls, text messages, and social media). God almost always speaks in a whisper, not a shout.

• GIVE GOD YOUR "YES" IN ADVANCE

The key to hearing from God consistently and repeatedly is simply doing the last thing he told you to do. The Lord entrusts those who can be trusted with more and withholds from those who squander the treasure of opportunities and instructions (see Matthew 13:12). Be ready to say, "Yes Lord, speak, your servant is listening" and "Here I am, send me" before the conversation ever takes place (Isaiah 6:8). Samuel had this kind of heart and preparation. As we develop a heart that is pliable, willing, and ready to move with God we can be assured that the conversations will increase as well as the clarity and certainty of what the Holy Spirit is saying.

- ## PLACE A HIGH VALUE ON HEARING THE VOICE OF GOD

  The things we value we will invest in and make sacrifices for. Samuel was willing to direct his life and future based on the Word of the Lord. King David said:

  "How precious to me are your thoughts, God. How vast is the sum of them! Were I to count them, they would outnumber the grains of sand- when I awake, I am still with you."
  PSALM 139:17-18

Today God is thinking about you! He has plans and desires for your future that He is waiting to reveal as you seek His face and wait to hear His voice. My prayer for you is that you would develop a passion to hear His voice at a level that every thought God thinks about you is a precious and priceless treasure. As you place a high value on hearing from God you will begin to invest more time, attention and even make sacrifices to position your life to say "speak Lord, your servant is listening."

MEMORY VERSE
"Whether you turn to the right or to the left, your ears will hear a voice behind you, saying, 'This is the way; walk in it.'"
ISAIAH 30:21

PRAYER DIRECTIVE

Ask clearly and boldly for God to speak to you! Pray for all other competing voices to be silenced. Pray that you would have a strong desire to live near the presence of God and never leave! Grab your journal and Bible, fully expecting to hear clearly as you wait.

THOUGHTS & NOTES

CHAPTER 7
THE ADVANTAGE

Today I want you to consider the privilege and power that is available to all of us through the person of the Holy Spirit! There is a clear and sequential promise that was given to the Church when Peter preached the inaugural sermon on Opening Day (see Acts Ch. 2). Within this simple and powerful verse, we find the starting blocks of the life of a disciple, and the invitation to live with a continual source of power and guidance.

"Peter replied, "Each of you must repent of your sins and turn to God and be baptized in the name of Jesus Christ for the forgiveness of your sins. Then you will receive the gift of the Holy Spirit."

ACTS 2:38

The gift of the Holy Spirit is both a baptism of power and a continual invitation to walk with the Holy Spirit as our friend and companion in life. It's not uncommon for people to view the Holy Spirit as something other than a part of the Trinity, that is, fully God as a person. We easily recognize God the Father, with our mental images of what "Our Father who art in heaven" could look like upon His throne. And of course, we know Jesus walked the earth in a body, spending time with friends and living life as one of us. The Holy Spirit has been described as a power, wind, fire, river, feeling, force, presence and many other things other than the third person of the Godhead.

He has a personality, will, and the ability to be our closest friend. When Jesus was saying His final goodbyes and commissioning His disciples to go into all the world, He told them that He would "send **Him**" and that "**He** will be with your forever" (John 14:17).

> *"I'm about to leave you and go back to join the One who sent me, yet not one of you are asking me where I'm going. Instead your hearts are filled with sadness because I've told you these things. But here's the truth: **It's to your advantage that I go away**, for if I don't go away the Divine Encourager will not be released to you. But after I depart, I will send Him to you."*
>
> **JOHN 16:5-7 (TPT)**

The advantage that Jesus was referring to is the ability of the Holy Spirit to be with all believers at the same time, releasing "the very same spirit that raised Christ from the dead" (Romans 8:11). He promises to be at work and walking alongside us every day of our lives. What a promise!

As we walk with the Holy Spirit, we will discover that:

> *1. He is our closest friend.*
> *2. He is our guide.*
> *3. He is the voice of God.*

For our time together today, let's consider the Holy Spirit's ability to guide our lives, leading us into everything that God has planned for us. This is not an unreachable state of spiritual maturity or a rare gift for a select few but is our inheritance and God's desire for

"There is so much more I want to tell you, but you can't bear it now. When the Spirit of truth comes (one of the names of the Holy Spirit), He will guide you into all truth. He will not speak on his own but will tell you what he has heard. He will tell you about the future."

JOHN 16:12-13

every believer, if we will simply walk closely with the Holy Spirit and prioritize His friendship.

Each member of the Godhead has a job description and attributes that are unique to them.

Let's think about what would be on the Holy Spirit's résumé:

- He was there at creation with Jesus and took part in creating the planet.
- He spoke to all of the prophets and performed all of the miracles in the Old Testament.
- He raised Jesus from the dead.
- He wrote the BIBLE.
- He brings us to Salvation, as Jesus stated, "No man comes to the Father, unless the Spirit draws them" (John 14:6).
- He releases all of the gifts because they are His.

One of the Holy Spirit's attributes or responsibilities is to give guidance and insight to those who know Jesus and long to follow him.

When we walk with the Holy Spirit, we can be sure that He will guide us into all truth, and if we are being guided into all truth, it means that we are being steered away from deception. You cannot be led to truth and deceit at the same time. You can't travel in God's direction and be lost or confused at the same time. You may not know everything that's going on, or where you will end up, but you will have a deep peace and confidence that it's going to be all good. Just keep following Him! The Holy Spirit guides us **into** God's promises and **away** from disillusionment and broken promises. He reveals God's plan for our future, thus giving us continual hope, vision, and passion as we move forward.

In light of these realities, it would be to our advantage to pursue a nearness and friendship with God the Holy Spirit.

The Holy Spirit is our guide!

"JESUS TAKING THE WHEEL" IS THE KEY TO CLEAR AND CONSISTENT GUIDANCE

Determine in advance to follow where He leads. Don't try to get God to endorse and bless a path or decision that you've developed apart from His clear leading and confirmation through His Word. Be completely vulnerable and humble before Him. This is a place of safety, blessing, and ultimate victory, even if it requires the temporary pain of laying down something or someone on the altar.

When God guides our steps, it will eventually and inevitably include a journey up a mountain of sacrifice and moments of letting go of the currently "valuable things" in our lives, only to discover the greater things of God on the other side of the test (see Genesis 22).

A PERSONAL NOTE OF TESTIMONY

When I first started following Jesus, the Lord led me to lay down a relationship I was in and give myself to Him alone until further notice. This was a difficult decision with a personal and emotional price tag included. By God's grace, I took this step of faith and trusted the Lord with my unknown future. Just six months later I would meet Donna, my wife of now thirty-seven years and the perfect mate and ministry partner for me. So, my experience for over three decades of following Jesus and building His church has been that every time God is getting ready to advance my life and expand my influence, it comes complete with a test of laying down some level of security or familiarity in order to enter the new season. We can all live with this confidence that the Holy Spirit will only lead us into decisions that will ultimately take us to God's best for our future.

TAKE A MOMENT

Consider the areas of your life that need clear direction. Is there a decision up ahead that you are uncertain about which way to go? Is there a relationship that you are not quite sure how to navigate? Whatever you are going through today, the Holy Spirit is available and willing to give you direction. Simply wait on him and ask in faith. I encourage you to write down your top three decisions that you need clarity on. Lay them before the Lord and ask the Holy Spirit to "lead you into all truth," and ask Him to "tell you about the future."

MEMORY VERSE

*"When the Spirit of truth comes,
he will guide you into all truth."*

JOHN 16:13

PRAYER DIRECTIVE

As you pray, ask the Holy Spirit to walk with you in a nearness and with a friendship that you have never known. If you have unknowingly neglected conversation and fellowship with the Holy Spirit, that can change today! First, repent of anything that might have quenched the Holy Spirit in your life (1 Thessalonians 5:19) and second, invite Him to speak to you today. Pray for clarity in your hearing and clear direction for every future decision. Know that the Holy Spirit guides you into all truth. Pray for a greater awareness of His presence and a greater activation of His gifts in your life. Today, may you be filled with the Spirit.

THOUGHTS & NOTES

CHAPTER 8
THE POWER OF WAITING

Have you ever met anyone who likes to wait? I haven't. DMV lines, traffic jams, and overcrowded restaurants all create feelings of anxiety and the sense that a waste of life is taking place. The feelings of anxiety or loss that are connected with waiting vary in all of us. Patience is not a personal strength for me and our culture does not help the situation as we live in a society that prioritizes expediting everything and has forgotten the value of waiting. Today I want to consider a different kind of waiting. Not the I'm bored, tap your foot, stare at your watch as the seconds and hours tick by type of waiting, but an intentional waiting that will cause something powerful to take place in your life!

Looking back, would you agree that the times of waiting have been the seasons of your life that produced something in you that would not have been developed any other way? The Bible calls this "patient endurance" and tells us that we need it.

"So do not throw away this confident trust in the Lord. Remember the great reward it brings you! ***Patient endurance is what you need now****, so that you will continue to do God's will. Then you will receive all that he has promised."*

HEBREWS 10:35-36

Throughout scripture we are encouraged to "Wait upon the Lord." Here's a sample:

> *"I remain confident of this: I will see the goodness of the Lord in the land of the living. Wait for the Lord; be strong and take heart and wait for the Lord."*
>
> PSALM 27:13-14

This concept of waiting that we see over and over again in scripture is not merely talking about marking time or holding out until God gets good and ready to move on our behalf. But this is an active waiting that will produce something amazing in the one who waits. It's important to understand and apply the meaning of this powerful Hebrew word, *qâvâh*, which means "to bind together by twisting, to be bound together with the object of our waiting, and to wait with expectation and hope."

The most accurate visual for this process that I can think of is to picture a three-stranded rope. One strand represents you, one strand is the Lord, and the third strand is the higher purposes of God for our lives. As we "wait," we are being twisted together with God's character and purpose for our future. *We are becoming one with the object of our waiting!* What an amazing picture! This kind of waiting is never a waste of time or a gamble as to whether our waiting will pay off.

As we wait, we have these sure promises:

"Indeed, none of those who [expectantly] wait for You will be ashamed; (humiliated or embarrassed)."
PSALM 25:3 (AMP)

"But those who wait for the Lord [who expect, look for, and hope in Him] will gain new strength and renew their power; They will lift up their wings [and rise up close to God] like eagles [rising toward the sun]; They will run and not become weary, They will walk and not grow tired."
ISAIAH 40:31 (AMP)

"The Lord is good to those who wait [confidently] for Him, to those who seek Him."
LAMENTATIONS 3:25 (AMP)

Today as you wait, expect renewed power and fresh strength. You are being bound with His purpose in such a powerful way that you will never be separated from His destiny for your future! This is the power of waiting. So, let's wait upon the Lord as we pursue Him.

Here are a few practical applications that have helped me to spend time in the secret place without becoming distracted or impatient in the waiting:

- **COME BEFORE HIM WITH NO AGENDA.**
  We all have our prayer requests, needs, and pressures that motivate us to pray hard. We need help, we need answers, and we need results. Jesus says He knows our needs before

we ever ask Him for help (Matthew 6:8). Try this in your *Pursuit* time today. Grab your Bible, journal, and a listening heart. Let the Lord know that He is your agenda. You have not come to ask, beg, plead, demand, or get something from Him, but to simply be with Him and hear his heart.

- ### DON'T SCHEDULE HIM TOO TIGHTLY.

    Something I have learned about the Holy Spirit… He's not in a hurry! This is more than the fact that He's eternal and lives beyond the boundaries of time. It's the reality that waiting, letting the peace of God rule in our hearts, and time spent alone with the Lord are the accurate weapons to defeat the enemies of worry, hurry, stress, anxiety and all other distractions that our busy lives are bombarding us with daily. I understand that we all have places to go and people to see but here's the challenge: set aside time where you can pursue the Lord and stay as long as you need to stay! Maybe it's a late nighter with nowhere to be the next morning, or a two-day prayer retreat at a cabin or secluded space. Perhaps it's as simple as blocking out an extra hour in your day just in case the Holy Spirit whispers… "Stay a little longer." This will almost always require setting the alarm an hour earlier and "awakening the dawn with your praise" (Psalm 108:2). Remember, power is released in the waiting; the soaring on wings of eagles comes after the waiting!

- ### PUSH SOMETHING ELSE OFF THE PLATE.

    I think this visual might help you. Your 24/7 schedule and the realities of time vs. responsibilities and activities and the need for 7-8 hours of solid sleep are a very real struggle and tension. This is your 'time-plate." You can cram only so much in that 24-hour slot and everything you commit to, make space for, or allow into your schedule takes up real estate on your 24-hour time-plate. So, in order to clear up some "waiting time" you will have to consider what needs to be pushed off the plate. This is between you and the Holy Spirit so I won't go down the road of possibilities and recommendations, but I'm pretty sure if you ask the Lord to show you what your wasted time looks like, and what could be pushed off the plate to make more time for the secret place, He will be faithful to show you.

- **ANCHOR YOUR HOPE TO THE SURE PROMISES OF GOD.**
  Waiting is all about hope. Hoping God will come through, hoping we will find new paths to walk, answers we are searching for, and the breakthroughs we need. Yet waiting with good intentions is not enough to secure the desired outcome. Proverbs 13:12 says, *"Hope deferred makes the heart sick, but a dream fulfilled is a tree of life."*

Hope can drag on indefinitely only to end in disappointment when our hope is anchored in our own emotions, unsanctified desires, or outcomes that involve the free wills of people who are not interested in the will of God.

There is a power released, and an intimacy discovered when we come to spend time with Him, for Him and Him alone!

"Awakening the dawn with your praise."

PSALM 108:2

I could share many stories along these lines but here's the point; if my hope is going be of the Psalm 23:5 variety: *"No one who hopes in you will ever be disappointed,"* then I must anchor my hope in the sure promises of the Word of God.

The very definition of Biblical hope is "an expectation based upon the reality of who God is and what He has promised." This is why it's so vitally important to make the Word a part of your daily prayer life and pursuit. **Get in and stay in the Word as you pray**: Read it, study it, meditate on it, listen to it and memorize it and pray it out loud. This practice will add jet fuel to your prayer life and anchor your hope!

So, before you set sail on the seas of new possibilities and faith adventures just be sure to "check your anchors," establishing that they are firmly connected to bedrock of the unchangeable Word of God and then get on the with business of waiting with expectation.

MEMORY VERSE

"The Lord is good to those who wait for Him, to the soul who seeks Him."

LAMENTATIONS 3:25

PRAYER DIRECTIVE

As you spend time with the Lord, let Him know that there isn't an agenda. You desire to know Him and His greater purpose for your life. Repent of running too fast, asking too quickly, and bowing to the pressure and pace of culture and a lifestyle that has forgotten how to wait.

Pray this out loud: "Father teach me to wait! Today you are all that I need, and all that I want. I have no greater need or desire than to sit at your feet becoming more like you. Today as I wait on you, I ask that I would be aware of, and bound together with, your greater purpose for this season of my life. But more than anything else, I want to spend time with you! You are enough. You are my reward. I will wait on you ... **AMEN**."

THOUGHTS & NOTES

CHAPTER 9
AGAINST ALL HOPE

"

Against all hope, Abraham in hope believed and so became..."

ROMANS 4:18-21

Some prayers seem more likely to be answered than others, while some situations in life appear to be beyond hope or reason. So why even pray? We come to false conclusions about hopeless situations because we often view prayer, and God's ability to answer prayer, from a finite perspective that is jaded by our track record of delays and failures. **God can do anything at any time and at a rate that is far more than we could ask or imagine!**

> *"Never doubt God's mighty power to work in you and accomplish all this. He will achieve infinitely more than your greatest request or your most unbelievable dream. He will exceed your wildest imagination! He will outdo them all, for his miraculous power energizes you."*
> EPHESIANS 3:20 (TPT)

Today I want to consider our prayer focus and intensity in light of the people and situations in our lives that appear to be "beyond hope." We all have that relative, physical condition, persistent bondage, or whatever else it might be that you've thrown your best prayers at for a prolonged period of time only to be mocked by the unwavering status of the situation and the strength of the enemy involved. Today I want us to pray "against all hope."

Let's consider the prayer life of Abraham:

> *"Against all hope, Abraham in hope believed and so became the father of many nations, just as it had been said to him, 'So shall your offspring be.' Without weakening in his faith, he faced the fact that his body was as good as dead—since he was about a hundred years old—and that Sarah's womb was also dead. Yet he did not waver through unbelief regarding the promise of God but was strengthened in his faith and gave glory to God, being fully persuaded that God had power to do what he had promised."*
> ROMANS 4:18-21

Is there anything more hopeless than being 100 years old with a 90-year-old wife while trying to hang onto the promise of a pregnancy and a promised child? I believe God uses this over-the-top scenario to show us how faith and persistence work in our lives. There are a few things from Abraham's story that can help us pray effectively and receive the promises of God:

- ### FACE THE FACTS

  Abraham was not in denial of the reality of the situation nor did he glibly confess that his impossible circumstance did not exist. He faced the facts and took his problem head-on. Don't be afraid to do the same. Tell God how messed up your situation is, how long it's been that way, and how unlikely it is that change will ever occur apart from His supernatural intervention. But don't stop there … go to the next step! If we state the facts without declaring God's ability to change them, then what some people consider to be prayer is just

"...And Abraham's faith did not weaken."

ROMANS 4:19

complaining. This never works out well (consider the children of Israel in the wilderness).

• DON'T WEAKEN IN YOUR FAITH

This part is on us. God will do what He has promised if we will continue to believe and not waver. But how do we not waver when circumstances around us are saying we should be getting weaker instead of stronger? Be filled with the Word and speak it out over the situation. When delays continue and our emotions tank, when people who love us have given up hope and told us to "move on," here's our to do: **hold your present circumstances up against the promises of God and then choose which one you will focus on and confess.** Faith not only comes by hearing the Word of God, but faith continues to come and increase by hearing, again and again, the Word of the Lord! (Romans 10:17)

• PRAISE GOD FOR WHAT IS COMING

"Abraham was strengthened in his faith and gave glory to God."
ROMANS 4:20

This is where belief turns into confession and our hope takes on a vocabulary that brings real change! This type of praise usually falls into the category of "sacrificial praise" (Hebrews 13:15). When we have yet to experience the fulfillment of the promise, a faith-filled sacrifice of praise is required. When we are between the prophecy and manifestation of it, this is where we worship, not based on what we see but upon the reality of who God is and what He has promised. Giving glory to God during extended times of waiting and unanswered prayer is all about focusing on who He is, what He has done and why it's likely that He will do it again!

TAKE A MOMENT

Stop and praise God for what is coming. Begin to lift the name of Jesus over that impossible situation and thank Him, out loud, for the impending breakthrough and victory. Tell God how big He is and how this situation is a little thing for Him. Remind God of some of His greatest miracles throughout history and then declare that "If He did it then… He can do it again." We give glory to God when we don't let go of His promises. We magnify or make God big when we give glory to Him during the waiting by declaring who He is and what He will do, long before He does it.

- ## LIVE FULLY PERSUADED

  Faith means, "to be convinced or fully persuaded." When we believe God and pray in faith, it means that we have come to a place where we wholeheartedly believe that God is going to do what He said He was going to do, no matter how long it may take or how hopeless the circumstances may seem. I challenge you today to become that kind of prayer warrior. Be a man or woman of God that lives fully persuaded!

  Before praying, I'd like to point out one more thing from Abraham's story. The Word says that Abraham was "persuaded that **God had the power to** do what He promised." Abraham didn't know when or how, but he **believed** God had the power to accomplish anything he promised!

This is the kind of faith that can hope against hope and pray hope into hopeless situations. Hope can be defined as a **"confident and joyful expectation of what is to come."** What is your expectation level during these days of *Pursuit*? What is your level of confidence and joy concerning what God is going to do?

• REVISIT THE ENCOUNTER

There were 25 years of delay between the promise and the fulfillment for Abraham, yet he was able to reflect back on key moments of encounter and promise as the years slipped by. He was 75 when God told him his descendants would be a blessing to every nation on the earth. Fast forward 24 years and Abraham is encountered again by angelic beings and the Lord himself to confirm that he and Sarah were only one year out from the promised son's arrival (see Genesis 17). I believe Abraham went back, mentally and emotionally, to that powerful moment of the original covenant, as well as the tent encounter to encourage himself and strengthen his faith. I would encourage you to do the same! Revisit those "holy moments" in the history of your journey with the Lord. Perhaps get out a journal and recount that moment He made you a promise about your future, called you to ministry, revealed that your family would all come to faith or whatever amazing promises you have been holding onto. As you go back to the place of encounter and promise you will find hope springing up again and your faith being strengthened to believe again for the impossible, to ... *"hope against all hope."*

"He was fully convinced that God is able to do whatever he promises."

ROMANS 4:21

PRAYER DIRECTIVE

Knowing that nothing is too difficult for God, let's pray some hope-filled prayers over hopeless situations. The enormity of our problem does not diminish His power or put our prayers in a "probably won't be answered" category. Go to the Word and find the promises that apply to your most hopeless scenarios and relationships. Hold those promises up against the facts and choose to declare the Word of God over them. Even if the answer to your prayer seems delayed, determine that you will wait in faith like Abraham living fully persuaded that ...**God can and will do it!**

THOUGHTS & NOTES

CHAPTER 10
SPEAK TO IT

> "
> *Jesus said, I assure you and most solemnly say to you, whoever says to this mountain, 'Be lifted up and thrown into the sea!' and does not doubt in his heart [in God's unlimited power], but believes that what he says is going to take place, it will be done for him [in accordance with God's will]."*
>
> MARK 11:23 (AMP)

Perhaps you've underestimated the power of speaking out loud to your enemies, mountains and seemingly insurmountable obstacles that lie between you and God's best for your life. Jesus was quite clear that the release-point of power is when we "speak to it." In your devotional time today, I want you to consider the power of audible, intentional declarations that are in alignment with the Word of God and filled with faith. Lift your voice to a new level of faith, intensity, and volume. Although mediation is powerful, it's not enough to meditate on God's ability to move the mountain.

It's not enough to call the intercessors or ask others to pray about your mountain (although the prayers of agreement are powerful). The operative words, the release point, the power moments are found in these words of Jesus …"whoever says to this mountain."

CHANGING SPIRITUAL AND PHYSICAL REALITIES

Let's consider how we receive salvation and become believers. Romans 10:9-10 says, *"If you openly declare that Jesus is Lord and believe in your heart that God raised him from the dead, you will be saved."* Belief without confession does not bring about supernatural change; neither does confession or declaration apart from a living faith; it takes both! This principle is first seen in the first three verses of the Bible and throughout the Word.

> *"In the beginning God created the heavens and the earth. The earth was formless and empty, and darkness covered the deep waters. And the Spirit of God was hovering over the surface of the waters. Then God said, 'Let there be light,' and there was light."*
> GENESIS 1:1-3

Three elements from this verse are present every single time we pray prayers that bring effective change:

- **THE MESS**
  "The earth was formless and void." According to the Amplified Bible, the earth was an empty formless waste. This speaks of the mountain, the trial, and the mess of our lives that looks beyond repair or change.

"It is written, 'I believed; therefore, I have spoken.' Since we have that same spirit of faith, we also believe and therefore speak."

2 CORINTHIANS 4:13

- ## THE SPIRIT

  "The Spirit of God was hovering." This speaks of our prayer time when we encounter and are empowered by the Holy Spirit. It's worth noting that the Holy Spirit is not opposed to hovering over the mess. God is not nervous or embarrassed by the messes in our lives. The Holy Spirit will come close and get involved with your worst-case scenario situations!

- ## THE SPOKEN WORD

  "Then God said." The Holy Spirit was hovering, but nothing happened until God spoke. This reveals our need to speak out the will and Word of God over the situation.

  When we truly believe what God is going to do, we will speak it out!

The reverse of that principle is true as well. When we allow unbelief, doubt, and fear to gain the upper hand, we find ourselves speaking in agreement with the circumstances and lies of the enemy.

Many years ago, I went through a prolonged trial of discouragement and confusion that led to depression and eventually despair. It was only by the grace of God and the prayers of people who loved me that brought me out of a very dark pit. As this dark valley became my reality I began to lose my song. My voice of praise and declaration of God's will and goodness went silent. Yes, I still loved Jesus and wanted to do His will, but somehow, I was slowly silenced by a very real enemy. ***The breaking point came when I made a decision, followed by a declaration, that "I would not go down in silence."*** In other words, I determined I would sing and declare my way out. This is an obvious and time-tested scriptural principle practiced by King David, King Jehoshaphat, Paul and Silas, and a long list of others. And sure enough... it still works! If your praise has been subdued, your song silenced, or your declarations diminished you can decide right now that it stops here! From now on, you can become a radical, vocal worshipper that changes the atmosphere and circumstances by praising God and speaking to the mountains in your life!

RECLAIM AND ACTIVATE THE WEAPON OF YOUR VOICE

"Beside the rivers of Babylon, we sat and wept as we thought of Jerusalem. We put away our harps, hanging them on the branches of poplar trees. For our captors demanded a song from us. Our tormentors insisted on a joyful hymn: 'Sing us one of those songs of Jerusalem!' But how can we sing the songs of the Lord while in a pagan land? (a time and place of bondage)."
PSALM 137:1-4

This is a very sad portion of scripture as God's people are taken captive and silenced. They willingly hang up their instruments of praise and forsake their songs of victory. This has always been the game plan of the enemy, to push us into a place where we no longer raise our voice of praise and our declarations of victory. When you are tempted to "hang up your harp" and forsake your song of praise, that's the time to shake yourself and resolve that the enemy will not have your voice! You will not stay silent. Be clear on this decision today and join your voice with the great Psalmist and warriors of the faith who declared:

"I will bless the Lord at all times."

"His praise will continually be in my mouth."

"My soul will boast in the Lord."

"I will lift up my voice."

> *"The dead do not praise the Lord. Nor do any who go down into silence; **But as for us, we will bless and affectionately and gratefully praise the Lord.** From this time forth and forever. Praise the Lord! (Hallelujah!)"*
> PSALM 115:17-18.(AMP)

Today, let's not complain or pray about our mountains; let's decide to be obedient and with childlike faith, sing over the battle and **speak to the mountain!** Are you ready?

TAKE A MOMENT

Identify and name the top three highest mountains, trials, or oppositions in your life. You probably won't have to think very long, as you've been staring at these intimidating mountains for a while. Once you've identified and named them, you will see them for what they are, a defying force of hell, an obstacle that is keeping you from God's call on your life, a demonic attack on your family, health, or emotions. As you enter into your prayer time, speak directly to those issues, and do what Jesus told you to do… "say to the mountain!"

SPEAK TO THE MOUNTAIN!

———

"O Lord, how blessed are the people who experience the shout of worship."

PSALM 89:15 (TPT)

YOUR VOICE OF PRAISE HAS A FREQUENCY THAT WILL BRING BREAK-THROUGH

Throughout the history of God's people in the Old Testament and New Testament, He has used the power of song, shouting, praise, and proclamation to open prison doors, collapse walls, terrify enemies, confuse armies, scatter demons and open heaven. This sound is key in the arsenal of the believer.

• **PASSION REQUIRED**

There are times when prayer is sweet and intimate, times when we meditate on the goodness of God, times when we weep in His presence, times to wait quietly and hear His voice but this is not one of those times. Mountain-moving prayer requires passion, declaration and, I believe, volume and intensity! You may want to shut the door, turn up the music, or find a place where you feel free to make some noise as you *speak to the mountain!*

MEMORY VERSE

*"I believed; therefore, I have spoken.
Since we have that same spirit of faith,
we also believe and therefore speak."*

2 CORINTHIANS 4:13

PRAYER DIRECTIVE

Today, we come in the authority of the name that is above every name, the mighty name of Jesus! We speak to the long-standing and intimidating issues that appear to be immovable obstructions. We speak to the mountains in our life! Take some time to find verses in the Word that specifically deal with your mountain. A simple word search on *www.blueletterbible.org* or *www.biblegateway.com* will get you started. Spend time speaking those verses out loud, letting faith fill your heart as you declare the Word, then speak to it! Do not be discouraged or dissuaded if you do not see immediate change, thank God that His Word is true, and continue to ask, seek, knock, and declare the Word of God until the mountains move!

THOUGHTS & NOTES

_____

_____

_____

_____

_____

_____

_____

_____

_____

_____

_____

THOUGHTS & NOTES

CHAPTER 11
DEAL WITH IT

Our spiritual voyage to maturity is a holistic journey. Seeing our outside world change, and having an amazing life of freedom and influence, always starts on the inside! Whenever we step into seasons of **Pursuit**, especially when it involves prolonged times of fasting and prayer, we will find that the work of the Holy Spirit quickly targets unresolved issues in our hearts and deals with the unhealed areas of our souls. At first, this can be discouraging or unsettling and appear that we are losing ground instead of advancing during our time of fasting but don't be discouraged! The Lord is simply preparing us internally for all He has planned externally. The greater work that we are all wanting to see God do in and through our lives will only get accomplished as the greater work of the Holy Spirit takes place from the inside out!

"Now to Him who is able to [carry out His purpose and] do superabundantly more than all that we dare ask or think [infinitely beyond our greatest prayers, hopes, or dreams], according to His power that is at work within us."

EPHESIANS 3:20 (AMP)

This is one of those "too good to be true" verses. Seriously?! God is willing and longing to do far beyond anything we can ask or think? Infinitely beyond our greatest hopes and dreams? I don't know about you but I can hope and dream up some pretty grandiose things and ask for some ridiculous miracles and outcomes. The operative phrase in this verse is, "According to His power that is at work within us." Another way to say it would be, "In alignment with, or an equivalent measure to the level of the Holy Spirit's work within us." **The key to seeing God move in power is to invite him to move in power within us.** Today, as we seek the Lord, let's consider a few areas that have the potential to limit or derail the greater things of God in our lives, and then ask the Holy Spirit to do an internal work as we agree to deal with it.

Following are three areas where we need to evaluate and then take any necessary action, to move into the "superabundantly more" program:

1. ELIMINATE ALL OFFENSES.

The sacrifice (or gift laid at the altar) is our prayers, worship, fasting, and pursuit of God in His Temple or presence. The instructions are quite clear. If while we are seeking God, we realize there are any unresolved offenses in our lives, we are to leave our "gift" or pursuit of God and resolve the issue first. One important nuance of this verse is that it's not even you that is carrying the offense or the grudge against someone else. He says that if we recall that "someone has something against you." So that means if we are unaware of any offenses or hurts we have caused or misunderstandings that are causing someone in our relational world to be offended, then we can go on pursuing God with a clear conscience, a clean heart and expect powerful results. But if we know or have a strong feeling that someone is

"So, if you are presenting a sacrifice at the altar in the Temple and you suddenly remember that someone has something against you, leave your sacrifice there at the altar. Go and be reconciled to that person. Then come and offer your sacrifice to God."

MATTHEW 5:23-24

offended with us, whether the offense is legit or they believed a lie or are holding a petty grudge over some trivial matter, that's not the issue. The issue and release point of God's blessing is when we go to them and do our best to bring resolution. **It's amazing how the heavens open up after we have done our part to resolve and release all the offenses in our lives**, so let's dive in and deal with it!

TAKE A MOMENT

Ask the Holy Spirit if there is anyone you need to text, call, or visit to work through some unresolved offense. You may not need to pray or wait on God for this one; you might know immediately as you read these words. So, here's the "to do," don't wait or procrastinate. Take action immediately. If you have already attempted to resolve it and they were unwilling, then you are free to move on and seek God with a clear conscience. If you feel you have done all you can in the past and an issue remains unresolved, perhaps the Holy Spirit would lead you to try one more time? No pressure here, but the Lord desires you to live free and experience easy access to His presence when you "bring your gift to the altar".

---

2. DON'T GIVE UP YOUR REAL ESTATE.

The Greek word for foothold is "topos" which means to give ground or real estate, to give legal right to inhabit. Ephesians 4:27 in the Amplified version says, "And do not give the devil a foothold (**an opportunity to lead you into sin by holding a grudge**, or nurturing anger, or harboring resentment, or cultivating bitterness)."

"In your anger do not sin." Do not let the sun go down while you are still angry, and do not give the devil a foothold."

EPHESIANS 4:27

"The unexamined life is not worth living."

- Socrates

As you wait on the Lord, the Holy Spirit will be faithful to bring to light all areas of real estate in your heart that you've given over to the enemy through resentment and bitterness. The Lord desires that you would live completely free of any and every trace of anything that may be holding you back from experiencing your full potential in Him, so let's deal with it.

3. KEEP NO SECRETS.
During these days of **Pursuit**, give God full and continual access to every area of your heart. King David sang, "Search me, oh God, and know my heart." This is an invitation to live a life of transparency with the Holy Spirit. God already knows our thoughts. You're not bringing him anything new, you're simply inviting the Holy Spirit to examine your heart (your thoughts, motives, secret ambitions) to identify and deal with any heart issues that are diminishing your life. As you grow in this area, you will discover a new and powerful intimacy and security in your prayer time. This is the beauty of living an examined life.

"God, I invite your searching gaze into my heart. Examine me through and through; find out everything that may be hidden within me. Put me to the test and sift through all my anxious cares. See if there is any path of pain I'm walking on, and lead me back to your glorious, everlasting ways— the path that brings me back to you."

PSALM 139:23-24 (TPT)

4. REFUSE TO GET STUCK!

Positioning your heart and mind to release every offense, forgive people quickly and not hold onto past hurts is the way to ensure you will continue to move forward in your life and ministry. Regarding offense and betrayal, Jesus made some clear statements that apply to all of us and we don't even have to believe them, memorize or quote them to see them activated in our lives. This stuff just happens!

"Then He said to the disciples, "It is impossible that no offenses should come."

LUKE 17:1 (NKJV)

"In this world you will have trouble."

JOHN 16:33

So, it's not a matter of whether or not offenses, betrayals and tribulations will continue to be a part of life on a fallen planet, but a matter of what will you do with them? As I look back on over three decades of life, ministry, and pastoring people, I've had my share of betrayals and wounds, as well as offending and hurting others. My observation is this: every time I've made a decision to forgive, resolve the issue to the best of my ability and release the grace of God into the situation, I've watched the Lord move me into new levels of authority, blessing and potential. The real issue is keeping our hearts clean and clear before God and able to always release grace and forgiveness to others.

MEMORY VERSE
"May the words of my mouth and the meditation of my heart be pleasing to you, O Lord, my rock and my redeemer."

PSALM 19:14

PRAYER DIRECTIVE

Ask the Holy Spirit to examine your heart and to reveal any areas where you might have given the enemy a "foothold." Ask the Holy Spirit to reveal any unhealed hurts or wounds you might have tucked away in the recesses of your heart. Ask him to show you any relationships in your life that might be damaged or anyone who is carrying an offense towards you, then make a prayerful and verbal commitment to deal with it.

THOUGHTS & NOTES

CHAPTER 12
PRAYING FROM THE PLATFORM OF VICTORY

We've all fallen into the trap of praying weak prayers of desperation that lack faith and confidence that God will hear and do something in response. We can easily get caught in a useless treadmill of prayer that does not produce results when we pray as if Jesus and Satan were battling over our future, and we are not convinced who will win. The very foundation of effective prayer realizes who God is and that He always responds to faith-filled prayers.

> *"But without faith it is impossible to [walk with God and] please Him, for whoever comes [near] to God must [necessarily] believe that God exists and that He rewards those who earnestly and diligently seek Him."*
>
> **HEBREWS 11:6 (AMP)**

Today I want us to seek God from a platform of faith and victory, knowing that Jesus has paid the full price to make us overcomers, knowing that He hears and responds to our prayers and confident that as we seek Him, during these days of ***Pursuit***, that an inevitable reward is on the way! This word "reward" comes from a root Hebrew word that means "wages will be paid for work done." **The rewards and results of diligently seeking God are sure and inevitable.** The key is praying from a platform of faith and victory, being confident that He hears us, and will do what he has promised.

As Jesus hung on the Cross, He uttered seven different statements or proclamations just before his death. His final words were "Father into your hands, I commit my spirit," and just before that moment, Jesus cried out, **"IT IS FINISHED"** (John 19:30). This was a shout or a loud cry of victory, not a moan of defeat or exhaustion. The phrase "it is finished" is one Greek word that is an accounting term as well as a proclamation of victory. When Jesus proclaimed these words, he was saying "It is paid in full," "It has all been accomplished," "The victory has been secured!"

> *"These words are not the cry of a defeated man, but it is instead, the shout of a victor! This is the exultant cry of one who has just won a great victory."*
> ALAN CARR

> *"It is Finished"* was a shout of triumph; the proclamation of a victor. The work of redemption that the Father had given Him was accomplished: sin was atoned for, Satan was defeated and rendered powerless, every requirement of God's righteous law had been satisfied and every prophecy had been fulfilled."
> JOHN MACARTHUR

As the demons of hell celebrated the death of the Messiah, they must have shuddered in fear when they came to the realization that they were actually pawns in the hand of God accomplishing the very purpose of redemption!

Because of this ultimate victory, we now pray from a platform or position of pre-purchased victory! When we understand and believe that "it is finished" it will change our outlook on spiritual warfare and the way we pray.

"We declare God's wisdom, a mystery that has been hidden and that God destined for our glory before time began. None of the rulers of this age understood it, for if they had, they would not have crucified the Lord of glory."

1 CORINTHIANS 2:7-8

TAKE A MOMENT

Ask your heart where you stand today in light of what Jesus has accomplished. Are you standing on a platform of accomplished victory or are your spiritual feet standing on a footing of doubt, fear, and uncertainty?

Here are three things that Jesus paid in full that can place you on a prayer-platform of victory today:

1. THE PRICE WAS PAID IN FULL TO RECONCILE US TO GOD.

> *"For God was in Christ, **reconciling the world to himself**, no longer counting people's sins against them. And he gave us this wonderful message of reconciliation. So, we are Christ's ambassadors; God is making his appeal through us. We speak for Christ when we plead, "Come back to God!"*
>
> 2 CORINTHIANS 5:19-20

The entirety of the gospel can be found in this one word, "reconcile." This means that through the Cross, we have been restored to favor with God. Today we do not pray from a place of trying to earn favor or from a place of working our way into favor. **The Cross has restored us to favor, and we pray as sons and daughters whose Father is longing to answer our request before we even ask.** This word reconcile also means, "to turn enemies into friends." This is

We have His full attention as we pray.

"Who shall separate us from the love of Christ? Shall trouble or hardship or persecution or famine or nakedness or danger or sword? No, in all these things we are more than conquerors through him who loved us."

ROMANS 8:35 & 37

amazing! We who were the enemies of God, because of the fallen planet and our sinful state, are now made the very friends of God! Let's see the Father through that lens today. He is our friend who has given us his favor.

2. THE PRICE WAS PAID IN FULL TO ENABLE US TO LIVE IN COMPLETE VICTORY.

I see far too many Christ-followers who are living in partial victory or even worse, living most of their life in a place of fear, discouragement, and defeat. "Believers" who experience only brief moments of victory, glimpses of what it's like to live as an overcomer, only to fall back into a posture of defeat and survival. The victory that the cross has secured for us is so complete that nothing can separate us from God's love! We are not only guaranteed victory but a continuous and undefeatable state of existence. To be "more than a conqueror" means we not only win, but it wasn't even a fair fight! It's an overwhelming victory, an irrevocable victory, a blowout, a beatdown of our enemies!

Today, are you living from a place of "it is finished," or are you living from a place of "I'm not sure I'll finish?" Let this verse resonate in your heart today and realize that, in Christ, you have already won and now you are merely praying it out, walking it out, and moving forward to a life of a continual overcomer.

3. THE PRICE WAS PAID IN FULL TO GIVE US "FULL ACCESS" TO THE PRESENCE OF GOD.

"Then Jesus shouted out again, and he released his spirit. At that moment the curtain in the sanctuary of the Temple was torn in two, from top to bottom. The earth shook, rocks split apart, and tombs opened."

MATTHEW 27:50-52

Historians will tell you that the veil was a curtain of woven material 30 feet wide by 30 feet high and around 4 inches thick. Josephus (a biblical historian from the first century) reported that the veil was 4 inches thick and that horses tied to each side could not pull it apart. Yet, when Jesus said, **"IT IS FINISHED"** the veil was ripped from top to bottom by the very hands of God, allowing all of us complete and permanent entrance into the very presence of God. The veil was not torn so that a few select people could get into the presence. The veil was destroyed so that the presence of God would be released into the world through His Church! The work of the cross solidifies your standing invitation to meet God face to face, have full access to His heart and thoughts and live in a perpetual state of friendship with God and dominance over your adversaries.

"Let us go right into the presence of God with sincere hearts fully trusting him."

HEBREWS 10:22

"So, let us come boldly to the throne of our gracious God. There we will receive his mercy, and we will find grace to help us when we need it most."

HEBREWS 4:16

MEMORY VERSE

"In all these things we are more than conquerors through him who loved us."

ROMANS 8:37

PRAYER DIRECTIVE

Ask God for a revelation of what it means to be "more than a conqueror." Ask Him to reveal the completeness and finality of His work on the Cross, then move into a time of prayer from a platform of victory and faith. Regarding the particular battle you are fighting, do some research in the Word and discover what God's will and final outcome in the matter will be, then use those verses as prayer weapons to fight with today. As you pray "your kingdom come, your will be done," you can be sure that it will happen. There is nothing that the demons of hell or even Satan himself can do about it! **It is finished!**

THOUGHTS & NOTES

CHAPTER 13
INCREASE/DECREASE

You have entered into this time of ***Pursuit*** because you have chosen to take on the daunting challenge of a 21-day fast. You are sensing a real and desperate need for more of God! This is a good thing! Spiritual hunger is a gift that we must steward. If we respond to the leading of the Holy Spirit to go deeper, taking on new spiritual territory, then He will continue to lead us further giving us greater spiritual hunger.

Today I want you to consider and pray for an increase of the activity and presence of God in your life. Consider and declare your need for an increase. As I said, you are doing this because you want and need more of God in your life - more healing, intimacy, miracles, breakthrough, finances, clarity, power, and gifting than ever before. The spiritual reality is **to see an increase a decrease is required**. God moving in and filling our lives with all that is "more" requires a displacement. When John the Baptist was at the peak of his ministry, Jesus' popularity and public ministry were quickly becoming the talk of the land. John's disciples were alarmed that they might lose their status and influence, so they came to John saying,

> *"Rabbi, the man you met on the other side of the Jordan River, the one you identified as the Messiah, is also baptizing people. And everybody is going to him instead of coming to us."*
> JOHN 3:26

John responded to their self-protection and jealously by letting them know that he was not the big deal, Jesus was. John was there only to prepare the way, and then get out of the way. John made this now famous statement,

> *"He must increase, but I must decrease."*
> **JOHN 3:30 (NKJV)**

The key to having more of God in our lives is the displacement of self, ego, and everything else that desires to be first. Fasting and prayer are the spiritual weapons that God has given us to accomplish this monumental task of defeating the "me monster." Fasting diminishes the soul and elevates the Spirit. Fasting reveals wrong motives and deals a death blow to our appetites and temporary desires. Fasting, with prayer, is the purest and most certain path to walking in the Spirit. Fasting and prayer brings an increase of God and a decrease of self!

Paul wrote of a very real spiritual battle, not with Satan and demons, but with our flesh:

> *"Here's my instruction: walk in the Spirit, and let the Spirit bring order to your life. If you do, you will never give in to your selfish and sinful cravings. For everything the flesh desires goes against the Spirit, and everything the Spirit desires goes against the flesh. There is a constant battle raging between them that prevents you from doing the good you want to do."*
> **GALATIANS 5:16-17 (VOICE)**

In the writings of John, we are commanded to, "Not love the world or anything in it" (1 John 2:15). This verse is not talking about the inhabitants of the world (humanity) or the beauty of creation (the planet), but is talking about the 'kosmos,' fallen systems, priorities and wickedness of a culture that exists for self and not for God. John goes on to say:

> "For the world (kosmos) offers only a craving for physical pleasure, a craving for everything we see, and pride in our achievements and possessions. These are not from the Father, but are from this world."
>
> 1 JOHN 2:16

TAKE A MOMENT

Reflect and consider how going after what you wanted, apart from the leading of the Holy Spirit, has only led you to places you didn't want to be, ending in frustration and futility. Then, meditate on those seasons of your spiritual journey when all you wanted was God's will, His nearness, and His highest call for your life. Would you agree that your "hungry days" were your best moments that led to the greatest seasons of your life? Thank God that there is more to come and our past delays and derailments in no way eliminate the possibilities of walking into all God has for us in the future. This season of fasting and prayer will set you on that path of new hunger for God, releasing new levels of success and fulfillment!

1. USE THE WEAPON OF FASTING TO DEFEAT THE ENEMY OF SELFISHNESS

King David said, "I humbled my soul with fasting."

PSALM 35:13 (AMP)

The "soul" is the seat of our will, emotions, and passions. Through fasting, we can diminish our own desires and receive God's. We dethrone our will and discover His will. We decrease so that He will increase in us!

2. GET LOW

Literally, bow down. One of the seven Hebrew words for praise in the Old testament is 'barak' which means to kneel down and bless.

> *"Praise (barak) our God, all peoples, let the sound of his praise be heard."*
>
> **PSALM 66:8**

Humility is an invitation to move into the greater things of God. It's up to us as to how often we take the "humble road" and make a greater space for God to show up in our lives. Bowing is a simple and profound way of humbling ourselves before God on a daily basis. As you go about your day today be aware of and take the opportunities, to take the low road, give someone else the credit , make it about others and think of yourself less, not less of yourself. Remember the pace that you move up the road to greatness is up to you.

> *"Come, let us bow down in worship, let us kneel before the Lord our Maker."*
>
> PSALM 95:6

Our thought life is the real battle ground.

"Humble yourselves [with an attitude of repentance] in the presence of the Lord, and He will exalt you, He will lift you up, He will give you purpose."
JAMES 4:10 (AMP)

3.   CAPTURE YOUR THOUGHTS
This is where the war for your future is won or lost. Variations of this quote have been accredited to different authors, but the truth comes straight from Word of God:

"We can demolish every deceptive fantasy that opposes God and break through every arrogant attitude that is raised up in defiance of the true knowledge of God. We capture, like prisoners of war, every thought and insist that it bow in obedience to the Anointed One."
2 CORINTHIANS 10:5 (TPT)

"Watch your thoughts, they become words; watch your words, they become actions; watch your actions, they become habits; watch your habits, they become character; watch your character, for it becomes your destiny."
RALPH WALDO EMERSON

Through fasting and prayer, we can take captive every thought that "exalts itself against the knowledge of God" that is, tries to sit at the highest place of our piriorities and passions. Once these selfish ambitions and rogue imaginations have been identified and brought down, we can begin to dream and meditate on the thoughts that God will give us for our future. These divine or "sanctified" thoughts become the runway for the increase of God's purpose in our lives. Today let's dream about what God wants to do as we get ourselves out of the way and ask Him to increase our spiritual hunger, our influence and our capcity to change our world!

MEMORY VERSE

"He must increase,
but I must decrease."

JOHNS 3:30 (NKJV)

PRAYER DIRECTIVE

What's your prayer posture? Some sit, some stand, some pace, some kneel or a combination of the above. Today I would ask you to bow low. Kneel or lay before the Lord in a posture of humility. Often during my prayer times or as I prepare to stand on a stage under the bright lights, I will lay on the carpet in my office, at the lowest elevation I can manage. I let God know how much I need Him to be big in my life today. Ask God to reveal anything that exalts itself against the knowledge and authority of God in your life, and then pray this out loud, "Lord, I ask that I would decrease and that you would increase. As I bow down in your presence, I am asking that my desire to be first would be displaced and that you and you alone would be on the throne of my heart. I want people to see you, hear you, and know you through my life, so I say, 'you must increase, and I must decrease' in Jesus name!"

THOUGHTS & NOTES

CHAPTER 14
GOD OF MIRACLES

" *Jesus Christ is the same yesterday, today, and forever."*

HEBREWS 13:8

Not wanting to deal with hope deferred and disappointment, I've often been guilty of praying small prayers, aiming low, and believing for too little. Yet, the Word of God keeps bringing me back to the fact that we serve an all-powerful God of miracles that wants us to believe for amazing, "only God" answers to prayer that will give Him all the glory!

Let's not allow our prayer lives to live in the lowlands of praying safe and no-risk prayers. For example, praying for a good parking spot at the mall or that the DMV line would be miraculously short. Today I want you to raise your faith by praying some big prayers. Let's believe for, ask for, and expect that the God of Miracles will do what only He can do in our lives!

A miracle by definition, according to *Merriam-Webster.com*, is "an extraordinary event manifesting divine intervention in human affairs." This supports the Bible's definition of a miracle. A concise description of a miracle, based on the three Greek words used for a miracle in the New Testament is **"an unusual event/ releasing supernatural power/ to confirm the gospel."**

As we pray and believe for miracles, we are asking for something beyond our human ability or capacity that will give glory to God and lead people to Jesus. We like to say it this way, **"ONLY GOD!"** Only God could have cured cancer, only God could have saved the marriage, only God could have opened the door. As we study miracles in the New Testament, both the miracles of Jesus and those in the New Testament church, we will find some recurring themes and common denominators of faith, passion, and desperation. There are many questions we could ask and explore about miracles, or the lack of them in our day, but I think the most productive endeavor would be to discover and apply some of the frequently found behaviors of those who received a miracle. Here's a familiar miracle, a snapshot of a day in the life of Jesus.

> *"They spent some time in Jericho. As Jesus was leaving town, trailed by his disciples and a parade of people, a blind beggar by the name of Bartimaeus, son of Timaeus, was sitting alongside the road. When he heard that Jesus the Nazarene was passing by, he began to cry out, 'Son of David, Jesus! Mercy, have mercy on me!' Many tried to hush him up, but he yelled all the louder, 'Son of David! Mercy, have mercy on me!' Jesus stopped in his tracks. 'Call him over.' They called him. 'It's your lucky day! Get up! He's calling you to come!' Throwing off his coat, he was on his feet at once and came to Jesus. Jesus said, 'What can I do for you?' The blind man said, 'Rabbi, I want to see.' 'On your way,' said Jesus. 'Your faith has saved and healed you.'"*

MARK 10:46-52 (MSG)

"Your faith has made you whole."

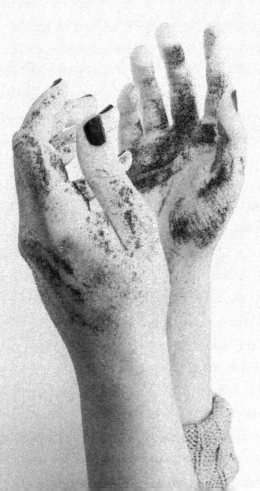

And there we have it, the miracle moment! A guy who has lived the life of a blind beggar is now seeing, possibly for the first time and following Jesus and his entourage down the road. But why did Jesus stop and heal Bartimaeus? There were thousands of sick and desperate people coming to Jesus. They lined the main streets begging for alms and asking for mercy, and yet, Jesus stops and heals Bartimaeus. I believe we can learn something from this story that will help to position our lives for an **"ONLY GOD"** miracle.

Jesus spoke the key phrase, "Your faith has made you whole." Yes, there are plenty of people that Jesus healed who had little faith or no faith. He even raised dead people without their permission or involvement in the miracle. Yet we can see from this story that **our faith and desperation can put a demand on the power and presence of God.** Here are some attributes of miracle-producing faith:

1. FAITH HAS A VOCABULARY

"He began to shout, 'Jesus, Son of David, have mercy on me!' Many rebuked him and told him to be quiet, but he shouted all the more."
MARK 10:47

It's worth noting that Bartimaeus didn't call Jesus the son of Joseph or Mary but used a title that revealed his faith that Jesus was, in fact, the promised Messiah. He believed that Jesus would open the eyes of the blind and unplug the deaf ears (see Isaiah 35:5). A vocabulary of faith declares who Jesus is and what God can do. So, here's the question: Do you spend more of your prayer time crying out, "Why God!?" or "Why me!?" than you do declaring who God is in that situation and explicitly asking for a miracle?

2. GREAT FAITH FREES US FROM PRIDE
(IT DOESN'T CARE WHAT PEOPLE THINK)

When Bartimaeus was rebuked by the crowd, he shouted all the louder and all the more. This is the point of faith, and or desperation, that pushes beyond our personality type or the intimidation and fear that would usually cause us to draw back and not make a scene. God does not call us to do things to embarrass or belittle us, but there are times when a radical faith will cause you to do things that pride and maintaining your self-image would never allow. This desperate and unashamed type of behavior is a reoccurring theme in the New Testament possibly the access point to "childlike faith."

3. GREAT FAITH CASTS OFF WHAT NEEDS TO BE LEFT BEHIND

In Bartimaeus' culture, beggars would sit on cloaks (large coats that served as a mat to sleep on and a blanket to wrap up in at night). Bartimaeus would sit on his cloak during the day begging for spare change. The cloak would have been filthy from lying beside the road day and night. This cloak or garment is a picture of our broken past. When Jesus told his disciples to call Bartimaeus over, Bartimaeus throws off this cloak, this identification and connection to a life of blindness and begging.

*"Therefore, since we are surrounded by such a great cloud of witnesses, **let us throw off everything that hinders** and the sin that so easily entangles. And let us run with perseverance the race marked out for us."*
HEBREWS 12:1

4. GREAT FAITH HAS A BEHAVIOR
(IT DOESN'T STOP PURSUING JESUS)

*"He **kept** calling out."*

By now, you have probably recognized a consistent theme in a life of ***Pursuit*. We never stop pursuing.** There is something about a tenacious, desperate, pride-abandoning faith that's determined to apprehend the answer. This is the kind of faith that receives a miracle. My prayer for you today is that you would be stirred in your spirit to believe big, ask big, and to quote the prophet Steve Perry, **"DON'T STOP BELIEVIN."** We are pursuing a mighty God who still performs miracles!

MEMORY VERSE
"Jesus Christ is the same yesterday, today, and forever."
HEBREWS 13:8

PRAYER DIRECTIVE

As you spend time with the Lord today, take some time to read a few of Jesus' miracles, and let fresh vision of what he can do fill your spirit. See Him walking the streets of Jerusalem and the back roads of Galilee. Envision Him calling blind Bartimaeus over, see Him healing the ten lepers, picture Him separating the crowd to heal the woman with the issue of blood.

Ask God for a tenacious faith that will:

- *Declare who He is and what He can do,* regardless of the situation.

- *Do not worry about what anyone thinks,* willing to lose pride and be as humble as a desperate child in order to receive the miracle.

- *Cast off what needs to be left behind* from the past.

- *Be persistent,* don't let people or delays keep you from reaching out to Jesus again and again….until the answer comes!

THOUGHTS & NOTES

CHAPTER 15
TURNING

We've all heard or used the term, "they made a real turn around." In essence, what we're really saying is that they repented. Many people misunderstand the full meaning and implications of repentance. **Repent means to have a change of mind, followed by a change of direction.** It doesn't necessarily mean that we'll feel bad about what we've done or that there will be tears of sorrow, although those things can be present in a moment of repentance over sin or failure. At salvation there is repentance from sin and a lifestyle change that comes (see Acts 2:38), but then there is an ongoing repentance or turning in another direction that keeps us moving closer and closer to God's heart and his desire for our lives. **This is what _Pursuit_ is all about, turning away and turning toward.** Today, let's consider and ask the Holy Spirit to speak to us concerning the areas of our lives that need a turnaround. The deeper our walk with the Lord becomes, the more sensitive we become to our ongoing need to turn our face and future toward Him and away from all that would diminish our lives.

> ## "Return to me, and I will return to you,' says the LORD Almighty."
> MALACHI 3:7

To return means to 'turn again, to change direction.' We have this clear and faithful promise that every time we turn again to walk towards God, He will respond accordingly (see James 4:8). If we have fallen into sin, we have a continual invitation to turn again and repent. This is an ongoing work of grace and a necessity in the life of every believer! The letters of John were written to believers, not to those far from God, and clearly show us what to do when we stumble and fall.

> *"But if we confess our sins to him, he is faithful and just to forgive us our sins and to cleanse us from all wickedness. My dear children, I am writing this to you so that you will not sin. But if anyone does sin, we have an advocate who pleads our case before the Father."*
> 1 JOHN 1:9, 2:1

Repentance and turning away from the sin in our lives is connected with an amazing promise:

> *"Now repent of your sins and turn to God, so that your sins may be wiped away. Then **times of refreshment will come** from the presence of the Lord."*
> ACTS 3:19-20

As this point in our devotional journey together, you may be several days into a time of fasting and prayer or recommitting your life to pursuing God in the secret place like never before. That being said, you may not be in a place of brokenness, sin, or failure. So, what we are going to read and discuss in this portion of our devotional may be for future use. Either way, I have found that Psalm 51 has been one of my favorite and most highly used portions of scripture in my Bible!

Following are a few verses from The Passion Translation. Read or sing these verses out loud:

"God, give me mercy from your fountain of forgiveness! I know your abundant love is enough to wash away my guilt. Because your compassion is so great, take away this shameful guilt of sin. Forgive the full extent of my rebellious ways and erase this deep stain on my conscience. I know that you delight to set your truth deep in my spirit. So, come into the hidden places of my heart and teach me wisdom. Wash me in your love until I am pure in heart. Satisfy me in your sweetness, and my song of joy will return. Create a new, clean heart within me. Fill me with pure thoughts and holy desires, ready to please you. May you never reject me! May you never take from me your sacred Spirit! Let my passion for life be restored, tasting joy in every breakthrough you bring to me. Hold me close to you with a willing spirit that obeys whatever you say."

PSALM 51:1-2, 6-7, 10-12

When we turn to the Lord, it releases the creative work of the Holy Spirit in our lives. There are three ways this takes place that God wants us to ask for and experience continually: **Create, Renew, Restore.**

"Create in me a clean heart, O God. Renew a loyal spirit within me. Restore to me the joy of your salvation."

PSALM 51:10&12

1. CREATE

This Hebrew word 'bara' means "to make something from nothing, to bring about new conditions and circumstances that previously did not exist." This word that David uses when he asks the Lord to Create a new heart is the same word used in Genesis 1:1 when it all began on this planet. I love the idea and potential of what can happen when we ask God to "create in us." We are asking Him to make something from nothing, to bring about new conditions and circumstances in our world and do something in and through us that does not currently exist!

TAKE A MOMENT

Consider what you need the Lord to 'bara' in your life today. What are you believing and asking for that is currently non-existent? As you pray today remind your heart that it is not beyond God's ability to create in you and through you... even from nothing! He is the creator and delights in making something from nothing in the lives of his children.... What a God we serve!

---

2. RENEW

To repair to make new again, the Hebrew word 'Kha-dash' means "to put a new edge back on an old sword/ to sharpen and polish, returning it to a state of splendor" (Genesis' Hebrew-Chaldee Lexicon).

Wow! Sign me up for some of that! We all need the creative, renewing work of the Holy Spirit in our lives today and every day. Psalm 51 shows us how to receive it. We humble ourselves and cry out to God for His transforming work of grace. During your times of returning to God He is sharpening your edge for battle and effectiveness in every area of your life.

3. RESTORE

Restore has the same root word as renew, yet reveals a fuller aspect and further application of what God does when we return to Him. To restore means "to bring back to its original state; to build again, to refresh, to repair, and **to bring back to full capacity, to take back what has been lost**." We have all gone through seasons of brokenness and failure where the enemy has gained access and taken something precious from us. This is where God's promises and power come into play and recover and restore what has been stolen.

"The LORD says, 'I will give you back what you lost... Then you will know that I am among you, that I am the LORD your God, and there is no other. Never again will my people be disgraced.'"
JOEL 2:25 & 27

One day King David and his mighty men were going to war against the arch-enemy and nemesis of God's people, The Amalekites. When David and his men returned home from the battle, they could see smoke rising from their home town of Ziklag. Their hearts sank as they saw this horrific sight. Their homes were destroyed, and their wives and children were taken captive. After weeping until they could cry no more, David inquires of the Lord as to whether he should attack the Amalekites in an attempt to rescue their families, to which the Lord says: *"Yes, go after them. **You will surely recover everything** that was taken from you!"*

1 SAMUEL 30:8

Perhaps that is God's word for you today! "You will surely recover everything that was taken from you." This promise of rescue and restoration always begins with a returning to the Lord. Before David recovered all, he first encouraged and strengthened himself in the Lord, and then he inquired of the Lord. He turned to God for direction and instruction, and this is the turning point that releases recovery and restoration.

MEMORY VERSE

"Create in me a pure heart, O God, and renew a steadfast spirit within me."

PSALM 51:10

PRAYER DIRECTIVE

Let's turn to the Lord today in every area of our hearts, minds and lifestyle. Ask the Lord to reveal anything in your life that requires repentance. Pray for the restoration of your own heart and life and then move those prayers outward, covering your family, your church community, and your nation. God has given us the authority and privilege to repent for our nation implementing 2 Chronicles 7:14 to see the restoration of our land. It all starts with repentance! *"...I will hear from heaven, and I will forgive their sins and restore their land."*

THOUGHTS & NOTES

CHAPTER 16
THE PROPHETIC EDGE

My pastor used to say, "The gift of prophecy is our home field advantage." So true! The ability to know what God is saying about our lives or situations, our calling, and the decisions that lie ahead enables us to pray with faith and accuracy, thus going farther, faster and accomplishing what God is speaking to us. The gifts of the Spirit have always been a subject of great debate, confusion and abuse as well as a blessing and powerful weapons for the body of Christ. My position on the gifts of the Holy Spirit is that despite abuse, hype, and frequent overdoses of "charismania," all of the gifts are for today and are a great benefit to the Church and the life of every believer. The 'win' for today's devotional would be to develop a stronger passion for the gifts of the Spirit and to grow in your ability to hear and speak out what God is saying, thus sharpening your weapons of prayer enabling you take some serious spiritual ground in these days of *Pursuit* and beyond.

Here are several ways you can gain, sharpen, and implement your prophetic edge:

1. GET PASSIONATE ABOUT THE GIFTS

"Follow the way of love and eagerly desire gifts of the Spirit, especially prophecy."

1 CORINTHIANS 14:1-3

The Greek word for desire 'zeloo' means "to be passionate, to strive after, to pursue with zeal and earnest pursuit." The reason so many people do not experience the gifts of the Spirit, or personally operate in them, is simply because they do not ask or pursue the gifts with passion. This complacency towards the gifts occurs either through poor teaching, lack of personal passion, or a mindset that says, "if God wants me to have them, He will give them to me," but this isn't what the Word teaches us. We must be passionate about the gifts of the Spirit and the Holy Spirit's activity in our lives.

TAKE A MOMENT

Ask God to increase the gifts of the Spirit in your life, especially prophecy. Ask for the gifts you feel He is leading you towards and stir up the gifts in your life that may be lying dormant (2 Timothy 1:6). During these days of **Pursuit**, the Holy Spirit desires to fill and ignite you with a fire and passion, so eagerly desire and run after the gifts.

---

2. KEEP COMPANY WITH SPIRITUALLY GIFTED PEOPLE

There are three dimensions of prophetic gifting revealed in the scriptures. Time and space do not allow for an in-depth study but here's the simple breakdown and big idea:

a. There is **the office of a prophet or prophetess.** (Ephesians 4:11-12, 1 Corinthians 12:28)

"When you assemble, each one has
a psalm, has a teaching,
has a revelation, has a tongue,
has an interpretation.
Let all things be done
for edification."

1 CORINTHIANS 14:26 (NASB)

b. There is the **gift of prophecy.** (1 Corinthians 14:1, 1 Timothy 4:14)

c. The **spirit of prophecy.** (1 Samuel 10:10-12, Numbers 11:29, Acts 13:1-2, Revelation 19:10)

Prophecy and other spiritual gifts are contagious! In other words, if you hang around with people who operate freely and powerfully in the gifts, you will begin to do the same, especially if you receive prayer from them. During your days of fasting, I would encourage you to attend or set up if necessary, some prayer gatherings where the prophetic are invited and released to do what they do. These gatherings have the potential to be defining moments and life and ministry altering encounters that set direction and release a new purpose for our future.

3. GIVE AWAY WHAT YOU WANT TO INCREASE IN

This is a spiritual principle across the board. If you want to increase in your finances, start with giving God what already belongs to him, the tithe, and then start sowing into the "good soil" of valid ministries, helping the poor and blessing any and every one the Holy Spirit nudges you to bless. And then see what happens.

If you want to increase the number of smiles and hugs you are receiving in life, it's quite simple, give more away. So, in regard to seeing the increase of the prophetic gifts and the "word of the Lord" in your life, start giving more of it away. Allow me to explain because this is not as complicated as you might think. Before I pray for people, I simply take a moment to ask the Lord this question, "Father, what do you think about them? What is in your heart for them and is there anything you want to remind them of?" As I start every personal ministry time with that brief prayer, with my motivation being simply and purely to see them encouraged and strengthened, God is quite consistent to drop a "prophetic thought" in my heart for that person. You can do this! We can all do this! Prophecy is not for the spiritually elite or an exclusive few, it's for all of us!

4. FIGHT FOR YOUR FUTURE WITH THE PROPHETIC EDGE

*"So, Timothy, my son, I am entrusting you with this responsibility, in keeping with the very first prophecies that were spoken over your life and are now in the process of fulfillment in this great work of ministry, in keeping with the prophecies spoken over you. With this encouragement **use your prophecies as weapons as you wage spiritual warfare by faith!**"*
1 TIMOTHY 1:18-19 (TPT)

Paul was telling Timothy that what God had spoken to him through the gifts of prophecy in the past, would become the current effective weapon that would enable him to battle well. This is a powerful and effective way to wage spiritual warfare. To take ground declare what God has already said about your life. Just as Timothy was reminded about the prophetic direction God had set for his life, I'm sure that you too have had some prophecies spoken over your life. I would encourage you today to get those out, dust them off, recall, recite and declare what God has revealed about your future.

5. DON'T GIVE UP ON WHAT GOD HAS SPOKEN OVER YOU

The most difficult seasons in our journey of faith are usually the delay between the promise and the fulfillment, the time between the vision and the fruition of the vision, the gap between the dream and when it becomes a reality. For Joseph it was many years of waiting and being tested by the very dream that God gave him (see Genesis, Chapters 37- 42).

"Until the time that his word came to pass, the word of the Lord tested him."

PSALM 105:19 (NKJV)

The same is true for us. The gap months or years, between the prophetic word and the time when it becomes reality, is where we need to fight the good fight of faith according to what God has spoken. Don't give up or back off, believe that God will do everything he has promised you.

I have carried prophetic words for years before they came to pass. Some I've carried for over a decade and there are a few I'm still believing for, contending for, and trusting God to fulfill. Perhaps the delays I have personally experienced were self-inflicted, perhaps there is a real enemy resisting the greater things of God in my life, or perhaps it's just not God's timing yet. Probably all three elements have some truth and influence in my reality. Here's the bottom line, I will not give up or back off from what I know is God's preferable future for my life; it has been revealed to my heart and confirmed through prophecy.

"For the vision is yet for an appointed time; but at the end it will speak, and it will not lie. Though it tarries, wait for it; because it will surely come, it will not tarry."

HABAKKUK 2:3 (NKJV)

MEMORY VERSE

"Follow the way of love and eagerly desire the gifts of the Spirit, especially prophecy."

1 CORINTHIANS 14:1

PRAYER DIRECTIVE

Follow Paul's instructions to Timothy and "battle well" by recalling what God has said. A personal practice that I would invite you try is this: I will often bring up word docs or get out journals of prophetic words that God has given me in the past and will lay them out in front of me. I will then take some time in prayer to remind God of His promises and also to remind myself of my prophetic potential and destiny. As you do this you will realize that God's words over your future are still alive and well, and you will find that your faith has kicked into a new high. Pray those God thoughts and prophecies out loud, speaking into reality what God has already spoken.

THOUGHTS & NOTES

CHAPTER 17
DON'T FAINT

"
And don't allow yourselves to be weary or disheartened in planting good seeds, for the season of reaping the wonderful harvest you've planted is coming."

GALATIANS 6:9 (TPT)

Hear it again: **"The season of reaping the wonderful harvest you've planted is coming."** Wherever you are on your personal journey of fasting and prayer you need to realize that prayer and fasting is a seed planting endeavor that takes time and a measure of endurance. Endurance is synonymous with biblical faith because faith waits, faith perseveres, faith sustains, faith believes into overtime, and faith never gives up. Through prayer and fasting we are planting, by faith, the seeds of our future reality. As we wait, pray, and worship the Holy Spirit waters the seeds of our prayers and then God brings the results. The operative phrase and key component to this process is clearly stated in the KJV version of Galatians 6:9, *"...we shall reap, if we faint not."*

The Greek word for faint, *'eklyō'* means "to relax, to weaken or loosen the grip and then to let go." The greatest enemy of seeing

God do 'the exceedingly and abundantly' in your life is spiritual fatigue and the ever-present option to quit in the middle. In today's devotional I want to give you some tools that will help you to battle weariness and to press on toward the full harvest of what you are sowing.

In Galatians 6:9 we are clearly commanded, "Don't be weary." So how can I obey those instructions and not be weary if I'm already weary? This word 'weary' is describing the point of giving up, to be utterly spiritless, to be exhausted to the place of letting go of the promise. If you were already at that level of weary, you would not be reading this and pursuing God. A Galatians 6:9 weary is a different kind of weariness than Gideon's army who were "weary yet pursuing" (Judges 8:4). Their weariness was a state of being, tired, thirsty and approaching exhaustion yet able to fight.

The key to not giving up in the middle of the battle is simply to not do battle alone...learn to call for backup!

In an earlier chapter we considered how King David and his men were exhausted after they discovered their hometown of Ziklag had been raided and their families were taken hostage (1 Samuel chapter 30). The point we made in chapter 15 was the reality that God will enable us to "recover it all." What I want to show you from today's content is our need to fight alongside others in order to realize the full return on prayer and fasting. We can see from David's battle that some days we fight for others and other days we need someone to fight for us. The secret to continued victory is to recognize what day it is.

*God has not called us to be significant
and powerful world changers apart from
vital connectedness to His body.*

*"So, David and his 600 men set out, and they came to the brook Besor. But 200 of the men were too exhausted to cross the brook, so **David continued the pursuit** with 400 men."*

1 SAMUEL 30:9

As the story plays out, we see that 400 of the men went in and fought for the 200 **who could go no farther**, yet they all shared in the plunder or rewards of the battle. So, the point is that when you are weary and can't seem to keep praying, fighting, and believing, this is where fighting alongside others who have your back will make up the difference.

Victory in spiritual battles requires community and carrying each other's burdens (see Galatians 6:2). Some days you need to call for backup and other days, you are the back up. This is God's design and keeps us from spiritual arrogance and isolation while creating humility through interdependence with the body of Christ.

Here are three effective ways to break weariness and continue your **Pursuit**:

1. REFRESH OTHERS

One of the best ways to break off spiritual fatigue, battle weariness and discover new strength in the journey is to take the focus off our battle and fight for someone else. Spend time praying for others, intentionally encourage someone else, and give something away. This sets things in motion to receive what we are in need of. If you will become an intercessor that spends consistent time in prayer for others, you can rest assured that God will move people to pray for you. This is an irrevocable law in the spirit.

> "The generous will prosper; those who refresh others will themselves be refreshed."
>
> PROVERBS 11:25

The Greek word for **'agree'** is where we get our English word **'symphony'** and means **"to blend, to harmonize, to be in unity and one voice."**

2. PRAY THE PRAYERS OF AGREEMENT

> "Again, I say to you, that if two believers on earth agree [that is, are of one mind, in harmony] about anything that they ask [within the will of God], it will be done for them by My Father in heaven. For where two or three are gathered in My name [meeting together as My followers], I am there among them."
>
> MATTHEW 18:19-20 (AMP)

God is omnipresent (everywhere all the time) yet there is a promise of a greater level of His presence and authority when we intentionally connect with other believers to pray. This kind of prayer is powerful and comes with an amazing guarantee that when we find this kind of harmony, we can "ask anything" and He will do it. This type of prayer requires a higher level of intentionality and an investment of time, but the payoff is well worth it.

3. CALL FOR BACKUP

There's a beautiful picture of intercession and partnership in prayer in Exodus Chapter 17. Moses instructed Joshua to fight the Amalekites while he went to the top of the mountain to hold out the staff of God over the battle. This is a clear picture of intercession and extending God's authority over the battles in our lives. As long as Moses held up the staff, the armies of Israel were victorious but when he became weary and dropped his hands (the intercession) they would fall behind in the battle. So, Moses had to call for backup. Aaron and Hur came to the rescue, holding up Moses' arms for the remainder of the fight as God's armies won the day!

> *"After the victory, the Lord instructed Moses, "Write this down on a scroll **as a permanent reminder.***"*
> **EXODUS 17:14**

God wants us to be permanently reminded that we cannot fight our battles alone and that we are not designed to endure prolonged battles without backup. Some days you are the arm holder and other days you will need your arms held high. The key to sustained spiritual victory is being ready and willing to step into both rolls. Let's not be too busy or self-focused that we are not ready and willing to be an Aaron or Hur for someone who is in the thick of it. And let's not be so isolated or suffer from spiritual pride to the point where we think we don't need back up!

MEMORY VERSE

"Let us not become weary in doing good, for at the proper time we will reap a harvest if we do not give up."

GALATIANS 6:9

PRAYER DIRECTIVE

After a time of worship and thanking God for all He is doing in your life, spend some time praying for others. Ask God to give you His heart or "burden" for someone in your life. A burden is not a negative weight that we are trying to shake but a gift from God to be stewarded. Pray prayers of refreshing and life over several people today, allowing God's heart for them to fill yours. Then, if you are feeling any level of spiritual fatigue or weariness, call for backup! Send a text, email or make a phone call and ask for prayer. Be specific and be sure to reach out to someone who you know will actually pray. Thirdly, consider who you could connect with at some point today to pray some prayers of agreement (Matthew 18:20). This does not need to be an hour-long prayer meeting; it could be five minutes on the phone, or a quick prayer meet up. As we use these simple, yet powerful weapons, I believe you will find new strength again and again and learn how to never give up!

THOUGHTS & NOTES

CHAPTER 18
THE REFUGE

" *Whoever dwells in the shelter of the Most High will rest in the shadow of the Almighty. I will say of the Lord, "He is my refuge and my fortress, my God, in whom I trust."*

PSALM 91

Over the past 17 days, we have discovered that faith-filled prayer is always connected to a promise, pursuing God always produces results, and seeking God ends in finding Him. This knowledge should ignite you with fresh faith to continue your journey as a life-long pursuer of God. Today I invite you to set your heart and mind to "live in the refuge."

I have seen many Christians exist without intentionally living under the shadow of the Almighty. You can confess Jesus as Lord and believe for salvation, while never actually living near His presence. The Lord invites us to a lifestyle of intimacy and protection. Today, as we meditate on Psalm 91 and the invitation to live in the refuge, we will once again see that there are decisions and action steps needed on our part in order to release a response on God's part. God has made some pretty amazing promises to those who choose to live in the refuge.

The word refuge *'machaceh'i* in the Hebrew, means "a place of shelter from rain and storms, a hiding place from sources of danger and falsehood, and a place of safety and hope where you find new trust in God."

Who doesn't want to live in the refuge of the Almighty? **This is a place of safety and protection, a place where hope and trust reside.** God is inviting us to take our time of *Pursuit* beyond a 21-day experience and make it a lifestyle of abiding under the shadow of the Most High.

Following are four ways to consider and apply Psalm 91:

1. MEET THE CONDITIONS

Most of God's promises are conditional, meaning that the fulfillment of His promise is contingent upon our involvement; God says, "If you will, then I will." An agreement and decisive action are required on our part. However, God also makes promises that are unconditional, meaning He fulfills His promises whether or not we agree or make a covenant concerning them. For example, "Upon this Rock I will build my church" (Matthew 16:18), "Behold, I am coming quickly" (Revelation 22:12), or "The God of peace will soon crush Satan" (Romans 16:20).

In Psalm 91 we can clearly see a rhythm and pattern of our *Pursuit* after God and His response in return.

*"Because **he has** set his love upon Me, **therefore I will** deliver him. **I will** set him on high, **because he has** known My name. **He shall** call upon Me, and **I will** answer him; **I will** be with him in trouble; **I will** deliver him and honor him. With long life **I will** satisfy him and show him My salvation."*

PSALM 91:14-16 (NKJV)

2. MAKE A DECISION TO STAY

To dwell means "to remain, to stay put, to sit down with the intention of not going anywhere soon." This is the same word used to describe people inhabiting a city. In the Book of Ruth, there is a beautiful story of heartbreak, loss, commitment, and redemption that plays out between a mother-in-law and her two widowed daughters-in-law. When it becomes obvious that Naomi will have to return to her homeland in order to survive, she encourages the girls, Orpah and Ruth, to return to their mothers' homes and find new husbands and move on with their lives. This was their response:

> *"At this they wept again. Then Orpah kissed her mother-in-law good-bye, but Ruth clung to her.....Ruth replied "Don't urge me to leave you or to turn back from you. Where you go, I will go, and **where you stay, I will stay**. Your people will be my people and your God my God."*
>
> RUTH 1:14 & 16

May we be the kind of worshippers who are not content to give the "kiss of worship" and go on our way but like Ruth we are determined to stay, to abide, and remain in close relationship with the Lord. God's promise to those who decide to "stay" is protection, rest, nearness and to be hidden in the strength of God himself!

3. MAKE A DECISION TO SAY

"I will say of the Lord,
He is my refuge and my fortress."

It isn't enough to know about the refuge of God or to meditate about the goodness of shelter. A spiritual dynamic takes place when we **open our mouths** and "say of the Lord." When we get vocal in our praise and declaration, He responds with the promised results.

TAKE A MOMENT

Take a few minutes and begin to "say of the Lord." This is a powerful practice that will take you into the very refuge you are declaring. Speak out loud who He is in your life, and picture that refuge in your mind.

> "Because he has set his love upon Me, therefore **I will deliver him; I will set him on high,** because he has known My name. He shall call upon Me, and **I will answer him; I will be with him in trouble; will deliver him and honor him. With long life I will satisfy him and show him My salvation.**"
> PSALM 91:14-16

Here are some lines straight from the Word to get you started. Let the river of praise and declaration flow from your heart.

"He is my refuge, My fortress, My deliverer...."

"He is my strong tower."

"He is my provider."

"You are my healer."

"God is the strength of my life... I will not fear what man can do to me."

"God is my comfort...."

"I Love You Lord."

"The Lord will sustain me..."

"God will keep me in perfect peace."

"The Lord is my safety..."

"God, I will abide under Your shadow..."

"My God will supply..."

"I will trust you Lord and I will not be shaken."

4. LIVE TO KNOW HIS NAME

This is a life of searching out and becoming progressively familiar with the character of God. As we increasingly learn the character and ways of God, He promises to place us in a 'high place' or a place of protection. I love the way The Passion Translation says it: *"Because you have delighted in me as my great lover, I will greatly protect you. I will set you in a high place, safe and secure before my face."*

PSALM 91:14 (TPT)

This secret place is the place of power! This refuge is the real estate of revelation. Under the shadow of his wings is where we find peace, perspective, and vision for our future. Oh, how the enemy, our busy minds and the frantic pace of our culture would try to hurry us from this divine destination, causing us to miss out on the very source of life and strength that makes for an abundant and well lived life! You will never regret time spent in the secret place. You will never want the time back that you spent at the feet of Jesus declaring who He is in your life. My prayer for you today is that you would grow to be and live life as a Psalm 24:7 person:

"Here's the one thing I crave from God, the one thing I seek above all else: I want the privilege of living with him every moment in his house, finding the sweet loveliness of his face, filled with awe, delighting in his glory and grace. I want to live my life so close to him that he takes pleasure in my every prayer."

PSALM 27:4 (TPT)

MEMORY VERSE

"Whoever dwells in the shelter of the Most High will rest in the shadow of the Almighty. I will say of the Lord, 'He is my refuge and my fortress, my God, in whom I trust.'"

PSALM 91:1

PRAYER DIRECTIVE

Today, take some time to tell the Lord your desire and intention to live under His shelter, to abide in the secret place, and to make your time and place of worship and intimacy with Him a priority. As the Holy Spirit leads you, make some determinations and commitments to increase your time in the secret place and to stay a little longer. Ask the Holy Spirit to reveal more of the heart and character of God as you wait on Him. Be ready and willing to slow down, wait on Him and hear His voice today as you abide in the refuge.

THOUGHTS & NOTES

CHAPTER 19
EXPECTATIONS

"In the morning, Lord, you hear my voice; in the morning I lay my requests before you and wait expectantly."

PSALM 5:3

Your level of expectation determines the level of your life.

Faith and expectation are often synonymous. Jesus said in Matthew 9:29, "According to your faith (expectations) so let it be done unto you." Today I want us to dig down deep and do an inventory of our hearts and faith level. Let's articulate what we are expecting God to do as we conclude this season of **Pursuit**.

Every year our church reads through a bible reading plan. I'm so grateful for Pastor Craig Groeschel, his team, and all the great folks at YouVersion.com for providing such an amazing resource that allows us the option of the audible version. As we cruise through the scriptures each year it's always a temptation to skip ahead when you run into a long list of genealogies and of course…Leviticus. Yet, tucked away in those long lists of genealogies you will find real gold, so don't read over them too fast.

Within the three-and-a-half-chapters, list of families and unpronounceable names in 1 Chronicles you will run into two verses describing a man named Jabez. His Hebrew name means grief and sorrow, beyond that, here's all that we know about him.

> *"There was a man named Jabez who was more honorable than any of his brothers. His mother named him Jabez because his birth had been so painful. He was the one who prayed to the God of Israel, 'Oh, that you would bless me and expand my territory! Please be with me in all that I do and keep me from all trouble and pain!' And God granted him his request."*
>
> 1 CHRONICLES 4:9-10

Back in 2000, Author Bruce Wilkerson wrote a New York Times best seller based off 1 Chronicles 4:9-10. While his book, "The Prayer of Jabez" was a bestseller, he also received some not so kind reviews from various theologians and critics.

No matter what your thoughts are on the book, the reality is that Jabez stepped up, believed for more, and asked for more than his family and predecessors! God was so impressed by Jabez' faith-filled-petition that He decided to include it in the inspired cannon of Scripture. I believe the prayer of Jabez is a valid contemporary prayer that I would encourage you to add to your prayer life, as it is in alignment with what the Bible teaches about God's desire to provide, expand, protect, and bless our lives... even beyond what we could imagine (see Ephesians 3:20-21)!

So, here's the big question today: **What are you expecting God to do in your life?**

Favor is a gift that we can ask for and position our lives to receive.

We never hear about Jabez again and perhaps we would have never known more than his name if it were not for this one phrase *"...and God granted his request."*

1 CHRONICLES 4:10B

God responded to his prayer of expectation and He will respond to ours. In fact, God considers this type of faith to be honorable. That is the word used to describe Jabez and is the same Hebrew word that is used to describe the weightiness of the Glory of God! I believe God is waiting for us to pray some weighty God-honoring prayers that put a demand on our faith and go beyond the norm.

TAKE A MOMENT

Write down what you are expecting God to do through this fast and in the next season of your life. Start with immediate expectations and then move out to a 5-year plan. As you write these down your faith will begin to rally around a clear and concise, articulated vision of what you are believing God for. Your expectation will become your prayer burden and the seeds of those prayers will begin the process of creating your future harvest. Obviously, all of our goals and desires must be in alignment with the word and will of God (see 1 John 5:14) or they will simply be futile fantasies (see James 4:3). I believe by this time in your *Pursuit* journey, you are hearing clearly and praying accurately, so don't be afraid to dream big and expect great things from God! Just like Jabez, **our expectation will become our request which will become our life's story!**

Here are four areas where you can expect God's best, and then you can branch out into specific prayer requests and personalized visions for your future.

1. EXPECT GOD TO BLESS YOU AND INCREASE HIS FAVOR ON YOUR LIFE

"Oh, that you would bless me..."
1 CHRONICLES 4:10

This is not a selfish prayer or praying outside the will of God. I would not recommend praying for suffering or pain, as life will supply plenty of that without asking for it. When favor comes things begin to click, doors open faster, connections happen that bring increase, and opportunities arrive without stress or self-promotion. Favor is a gift that we can ask for and position our lives to receive.

2. EXPECT GOD TO INCREASE YOUR INFLUENCE AND YOUR "TERRITORY"

"... that you would enlarge my territory..."
1 CHRONICLES 4:10

Pray this over your finances, your business ventures, your real estate and your church. We are asking God for more influence in our city, more territory where the kingdom of God has come, and His will to be done. The way this happens corporately, is as individual believers who are vitally connected to the local church expand and experience increase. Our blessing and expansion are always for a purpose bigger than us.

3. EXPECT GOD TO GIVE YOU GUIDANCE AND CLARITY FOR THE FUTURE

"... and that your hand would be with me."
1 CHRONICLES 4:10

God's hand speaks of His guidance and His direction. Sometimes He leads, other times He points and ask us to step out in faith. Believe that God is going to give you specific, detailed, and clear guidance as you take some big faith steps into the future. Remember that we need to give Him a reason to bring fresh guidance. "You can't steer a parked car," so let's move forward in expectancy.

4. EXPECT GOD TO KEEP YOU FROM TEMPTATION, SIN AND FAILURE

> *".... That you would keep me from evil so that it does not hurt me!"*

1 CHRONICLES 4:10

Jabez was not asking for a trouble-free world but simply praying a form of the prayer that Jesus would teach his disciples to pray nearly 1,000 years later... "and lead us not into temptation but deliver us from evil" (Matthew 6:13). Perhaps Jabez knew intuitively that with prosperity and favor comes temptation and persecution, so he is asking for protection in advance. I would advise we do the same. As you pray "lead us not into temptation" believe and expect God to do just that. God wants to put you on a broad and illuminated path where you won't stumble.

> *"The path of the righteous is like the morning sun, shining ever brighter till the full light of day."*

PROVERBS 4:18

As you do these things be sure to align your expectations with the Word, trust God's timing to fulfill them, and then wait in faith until. This is the life of expectancy that produces results!

MEMORY VERSE
"None of those who expectantly wait for you will be ashamed."

PSALM 25:3 (AMP)

PRAYER DIRECTIVE

Today I would encourage you to split up your prayer time into four or five sections:

- *Start with thanksgiving and worship.* Spend time just loving Jesus.

- *Journal your expectations* and what you are believing God for through this ***Pursuit***. Take your time and let faith and the Spirit of God move in on this moment. Some of what you write down may seem far bigger than what you've ever considered, that's ok!

- *Build your request on the Word!* If you have time, you may want to find some verses in the Bible that back up your request. This will add faith and clarity to you petitions. *Biblegateway.com* and *Blueletterbible.org* are a couple of great resources for researching scripture.

- *Speak out your future.* This is where we, by faith, begin to ask boldly and declare clearly what God is going to do in the future. Let your expectations of a faith-filled future turn into sound waves that have the potential to create a spiritual reality.

- *End with worship.* Thank God in advance for what He is going to do in the days to come… then go have a powerful day filled with expectation!

THOUGHTS & NOTES

CHAPTER 20
EITHER WAY WE WIN

> "
> *We long to see you passionately advance until the end and you find your hope fulfilled. So, don't allow your hearts to grow dull or lose your enthusiasm, but follow the example of those who fully received what God has promised because of their **strong faith** and **patient endurance.**"*

HEBREWS 6:11-12 (TPT)

Faith has an attitude. Faith has a vocabulary and faith has a resilience that cannot be quenched by delays, distractions, or even the silence of heaven. Today I want to stretch your faith to believe and pray beyond your current view of what you see. I want you to infuse your prayer life with patient endurance. It is often said, "We are playing the long game" in this life of **Pursuit**. Some of what we pray and believe for happens immediately, while some seeds of prayer breakthrough in the next season of our lives, and then there are the prayers that are invested in the next generation where we can only glimpse the results by faith. **Remember this: prayer is eternal, and every prayer offered in faith produces results and will be rewarded, even if it doesn't happen on our time frame or our watch!**

Hebrews chapter 11, often referred to as the "Great Faith" chapter in your Bible, is full of great men and women who believed God and accomplished mighty things through faith. However, there is a delineation. In verse 35, there's a slight shift that presents a level of faith that most of us are unwilling to consider, much less live out.

> *"By faith these people overthrew kingdoms, ruled with justice, and received what God had promised them. They shut the mouths of lions, quenched the flames of fire, and escaped death by the edge of the sword. Their weakness was turned to strength. They became strong in battle and put whole armies to flight. Women received their loved ones back again from death. **But others** were tortured, refusing to turn from God in order to be set free. They placed their hope in a better life after the resurrection. Some were jeered at, and their backs were cut open with whips. Others were chained in prisons. Some died by stoning, some were sawed in half, and others were killed with the sword. Some went about wearing skins of sheep and goats, destitute and oppressed and mistreated!"*
>
> HEBREWS 11:33-37

Time out, are we talking about the same kind of faith? Do you mean the faith that saw the dead raised back to life is the same faith

"These were the true heroes, commended for their faith, yet they lived in hope without receiving the fullness of what was promised them."

HEBREWS 11:39 (TPT)

that gets you sawed in half? How can that even be possible? Here's the answer and the reality, **great faith is vitally connected to an eternal purpose.** It's a commitment to trust God no matter the outcome. The same great faith that Daniel displayed that caused the mouths of lions to be shut, caused others to willingly walk to their deaths to be eaten by lions in the arenas in Rome.

I'm not trying to be morbid, discouraging, or depressing in pointing out this unique level of faith, but here's what we need to understand. **We need to pray, believe, stand in faith, and trust God while embracing the fact that the outcomes, timelines, and the ultimate results belong to the Lord.** Great faith continues to pray and believe even when we're unsure of when or how the answer will come.

Here are three ways that you can live with great faith regardless of the timelines and outcome:

1. BE CLEAR ON AND DETERMINED IN WHAT YOU WILL NEVER QUIT PRAYING FOR. DETERMINE NEVER TO STOP CONTENDING AND PRAYING FOR YOUR DESIRED OUTCOME.

If you are praying for unsaved friends and family members, never quit! If you are praying for a move of God in your local community or state, never quit. If you are believing for anything that is based in the Word and clearly the will of God, determine to "pray until." This is the very nature of great faith.

TAKE A MOMENT

Consider and then write down a list of people, situations, and outcomes that you will never quit praying for. Keep this as a petition and a reminder of your resolve. From time to time, pull this list out and let your resilient faith ignite with fresh fire.

---

2. BE CONFIDENT IN GOD'S REWARD SYSTEM.

Jesus was very clear:

"Ask and keep on asking and it will be given to you; seek and keep on seeking and you will find; knock and keep on knocking and the door will be opened to you."
MATTHEW 7:7 (AMP)

*"Without faith it is impossible to please God, because anyone who comes to him must believe that he exists and that **he rewards those who earnestly seek him.**"*
HEBREWS 11:6

*"For God is not unjust, **He will not forget your work and labor of love** which you have shown toward His name."*
HEBREWS 6:10

Faith-infused prayer time is never a waste of time! Wasted time is the time we spend trying to work things out in our own strength and human strategies, apart from the wisdom of God and active faith. We must live with a clear understanding of the sure promise of God that "if we seek him, we will find him" (Jeremiah 29:13).

3. BE WILLING TO INVEST YOUR LIFE, PRAYERS, AND PASSION INTO SOMETHING THAT YOU MAY DIE STILL BELIEVING FOR.

Twenty-two years ago, we planted the church I now pastor. Since the birth of our church, we have believed, fasted, prayed, contended, and prophesied for a historic move of God in our state. I am convinced that there is a great move of the Holy Spirit and revival yet to be released in California and our nation. I believe that the "Jesus Movement" of the late '60s and '70s was not the church's greatest days or high-water mark for our state. For over 30 years I have fasted and prayed, along with thousands of other believers, for a "Jesus Movement Part Two!" We are looking for an outpouring of the Holy Spirit that is unprecedented in its scope and historic in its nature. I still believe that God saves the best wine for last and that the latter rain spoke of in Joel Chapter 2, will intensify not diminish, before Jesus returns for His Bride.

Now if you do not share my hope or perspective on this, that's all right, the point I'm trying to make here is this: **I will keep praying and believing even if it happens after my watch is over.** I'm ok sowing years of prayer into a coming harvest that I may only see by faith. I do, however, believe I will see it in my lifetime, but either way, I won't be detoured, discouraged, or disillusioned if I don't see it. This is the nature of faith.

"What if I believe, pray, don't give up and it doesn't happen?"

Just remember, **either way we win!** This type of prayer life connects us to eternity and the purposes of God and has a generational continuance. This perspective is true evidence of great faith.

My Pastor, Wendell Smith, was one of the greatest men of faith I've ever had the privilege of knowing. He believed big, prayed big, and, in the wake of his great faith, influenced thousands of people to do the same. Yet, he battled cancer for six years and went to be with Jesus at the young age of 60. A couple of his great statements that he often spoke out during his final days were, "Let's finish strong," and "Either way we win!" What an amazing and accurate perspective! To live with the realization that life is but a vapor, faith is eternal, and believing God no matter the outcome, is the evidence of the highest level of faith. He wrote a book called "Great Faith," which he lived out and left as a legacy that is still growing and influencing multitudes! Pastor Wendell's faith and the fruit of his life have far outlived him, multiplying exponentially in the lives of thousands of believers, leaders, and pastors. I would be one of those.

"Without faith it is impossible to please God, because anyone who comes to him must believe that he exists and that he rewards those who earnestly seek him."

HEBREWS 11:6

PRAYER DIRECTIVE

Let's pray some "long-game-prayers." Write down some petitions that you believe God for and are willing to hold onto and pray them into existence even if it takes the rest of your life. As you pray, ask the Lord for a new dose of patient endurance. Ask for a new revelation of the eternal nature of faith-filled prayers and for the ability to join with those in Hebrews Chapter 11 who were *"confidently looking forward to a city with eternal foundations, a city designed and built by God."*

THOUGHTS & NOTES

THOUGHTS & NOTES

_____

_____

_____

_____

_____

_____

_____

_____

_____

_____

CHAPTER 21
NAVIGATING YOUR BEST LIFE

> "
> *Since we are living by the Spirit,*
> **let us follow the Spirit's leading**
> *in every part of our lives.*"
>
> GALATIANS 5:25

I love when people say, "I'm living my best life." I know that can mean something different for everyone and depending on who is saying it, can be subjective as to the level of truth involved. The concept and goal are admirable and is the thesis of today's devotional. I believe God is inviting you to navigate and **live your best life**. I would define that preferable future as being led by the Spirit of God while learning to recognize and respond to divine opportunities.

Through this season of *Pursuit* God has been positioning your heart and mind to move through new doors, stepping into the best season of your life. This will require making consistent decisions that are in alignment with His will for your future. Research from Columbia University has found that the average person makes 70 conscious decisions per day, amounting to 25,550 decisions made a year! It's those decisions that lead us to varying destinations and determine the outcomes of our life.

A series of minor decisions end up creating a major course for our lives. A simple decision like, "Should I sleep in or get up and pray?" won't yield obvious results either way over the course of a day but over the course of years it will define a destination. Here's one we can all relate to: "Should I eat fast food or get the green shake?" Again, there isn't an immediate consequence or reward connected to this minor decision, but ten years of unhealthy eating and drinking will determine a destination.

In Deuteronomy 30, God invites an entire nation to step through a door of obedience in order to live a life of blessing but in order to receive that life of blessing changes were required.

> *"Today I have given you the choice between life and death, between blessings and curses. Now I call on heaven and earth to witness the choice you make. Oh, that you would choose life, so that you and your descendants might live!"*
>
> **DEUTERONOMY 30:19-20**

Today I want to give you some thoughts about the nature of doors and how to navigate through them in order to live your best life.

THE NATURE OF DOORS

1. NEW DOORS ARE AN INVITATION, NOT A SOVEREIGN ABSOLUTE.

Many people get this wrong. Believers and non-believers alike can develop a "sloppy sovereignty theology" where God gets blamed for decisions he was not consulted in and results he never orchestrated. God is not micro-managing every turn

When Jesus called
His disciples,
it was an invitation,
not a sovereign
mandate.

and decision of our lives but has given us a free will and the opportunity to seek wisdom, call out for understanding, and follow the leading of His Spirit. How many times have you heard people say "everything happens for a reason" implying there is a sovereign destiny involved even in poor decisions, when in fact the "reason" many things happen is simply because we did not consult or involve God in the process.

There is an identical invitation that happened in Mark 7 in the story of "The Rich Young Ruler." A man asks Jesus what he needs to do in order to inherit eternal life. To which Jesus replies, "leave your possessions behind and come and follow me" (Luke 18:22). The young ruler decides to pass on this "open door invitation" and we never hear of him again. This was a sincere invitation from Jesus, not a trick question or an attempt to make him stumble. Today the Lord stands at the doors of your life and knocks, He never barges in or demands control.

2. NEW DOORS HAVE AN EXPIRATION DATE (THE KAIROS MOMENT).

I want you to get this visual: Life is a highway and you are moving quickly down it. On this highway are on-ramps and off-ramps. You are passing by many doors or "on-ramps" that will lead you to a greater, broader, more fulfilling future, but timing is of the essence. Many people look at the invitations and opportunities God offers them like a buffet, in that "they will just lay there under the warm lights until I'm ready for them" And it's not true! There is a "now window of time" There is a moment to take the on-ramp to the greater future God is presenting to you. Jesus approached Jerusalem and He wept over her as He said …

*"Oh Jerusalem... if you only would have only known the things, I'm trying to bring to you, but now they are hidden from your eyes... because you did not recognize the **time (Kairos) of your visitation."***

LUKE 19:44

Remember, navigating your best life is more like a highway than a buffet!

This Greek word kairos meaning "time" speaks of a season of opportunity and a window of divine favor.

Esther had an opportunity to be the hero for the nation of Israel by stepping through a door of divine purpose (see Esther Chapter 4 for context). As Esther's uncle, Mordecai, was coaching her through this difficult yet opportune season Esther battled with the scope of the decision she would have to make. The idea of being the messenger that would go before the king and ask for the deliverance for an entire nation at such a young age was overwhelming. So, Mordecai said, "If you remain silent at this time, relief and deliverance for the Jews will arise from another place, but who knows… perhaps you have come into the kingdom for such a time as this?" (Esther 4:14)

The window of time was short, the opportunity was right in front of her; Esther stepped up and became a history maker!

3. NEW DOORS COME COMPLETE WITH NEW CHALLENGES.

Just because a divine opportunity arrives and a new door is opened, doesn't mean that it's all going to be smooth sailing and opposition free. Many times, navigating through a new door will lead us into a greater test of our faith. The Bible is full of examples such as Joseph (see Genesis Ch. 37-42). He obeyed the call of God on his life but ended up being accused of a crime he didn't commit and ends up in prison. And yet, at the end of Joseph's life the fulfillment was well worth the price he paid! This will be true of your journey as well.

The apostle Paul said it this way: *"For a great and effective door has opened to me, and **there are many adversaries**."*
1 CORINTHIANS 16:9

Don't let potential resistance or temporary difficulty keep you from moving through the doors that God is opening for you! Your best life is on the other side of the temporary delays and the battles that you are sure to win if you will continue to navigate with God!

4. NEW DOORS ALWAYS MOVE US INTO A PREFERABLE FUTURE REGARDLESS OF DELAYS AND BATTLES.

God never invites you into something that diminishes your life! He came to give you an abundant life, not a diminished life. I would encourage you to move into your future with faith and a willingness to step through the new doors that are now opening. Just like God's invitation to Abraham, God is inviting you to trust him with your unknown future.

*"Faith motivated Abraham to obey God's call and leave the familiar to discover the territory he was destined to inherit from God. So, he left with only a promise and **without even knowing ahead of time where he was going.**"*
HEBREWS 11:8 (TPT)

If we are going to find out what's on the other side of an open door, we are going to have to walk through it. There isn't a brochure to explain where a walk of faith will take you or a 5-year plan that you can sign off on. You simply have to move with God. Be willing to leave the secure and the predictable for a chance to walk into the greater things God has beyond the open door.

TAKE A MOMENT

Consider the doors that are opening for you through this season of **Pursuit**. Ask the Lord to make them clear and then write down the impressions of your heart. What off-ramps and on-ramps are becoming apparent? What does He want you to leave in order to move into the better version of your future? What invitations are being extended to you? Generosity is an invitation, serving is an invitation, connecting in a community group is an invitation, leading in a greater capacity is an invitation. What are yours?

APPLICATION

It is the same for all of us. From Abraham, to Paul, to Esther, to you, to me. **If we are going to navigate our best lives it will require obedience and movement!** These first three words are the key to navigation.

"So, Abram departed
as the Lord had instructed."

GENESIS 12:4

MEMORY VERSE

*"Since we are living by the Spirit,
let us follow the Spirit's leading
in every part of our lives."*

GALATIANS 5:25

PRAYER DIRECTIVE

Let's prepare our hearts to give God our yes and to be willing to move through the open doors, even if like Abraham, we don't know where we're going. Pray for and pursue a pliable, willing heart of faith that will move with God quickly and without reluctance or doubt. A heart that will give God a yes before He ever asks you to move. Ask the Lord to clarify and illuminate the doors he is opening right now in your life and thank Him that your best days are ahead. Today you are living your best life!

THOUGHTS & NOTES